GAME FISH

OF NORTH AMERICA

GAME FISH
OF NORTH AMERICA

SILVIO CALABI

THE WELLFLEET PRESS

WELLFLEET

Editorial Director: Frank Oppel
Design Director: Tony Meisel
Origination by Regent Publishing Services, Ltd.
Printed by Leefung-Asco Printers, Ltd.

Manufactured in Hong Kong.

ISBN: 1-55521-275-1

Contents

Introduction

IT WAS IN POSTWAR EUROPE that I arrived on the fishing scene—hardly more than a toddler, strapped securely into a kiddie seat on the back of my uncle's bicycle. Lashed to the bike behind me was always a live bucket, a copper-colored thing with a hinged top and air holes, which was empty when we set out to go fishing but that must have been hell's own headache for my uncle to pedal back home when it was full of water and fish. Especially with a cane pole clamped to each handlebar in his fingers and a three-year-old nephew riding caboose.

This was Switzerland, where no road stays on the level for long.

We'd wobble down the lane and around a few bends to where a wooden bridge spanned a minor stream, and there we'd dismount. My uncle filled the live well and set it in the nearshore current, so water would bubble through the holes, and then we'd get down to business. He kept a small hunk of cheese at the bridge, out of sight on a beam, for bait; I had to lie on my stomach next to one of the railing uprights and reach down and under for it. Wonderfully scary. It wasn't the Swiss cheese we know, for it could be rolled into sticky balls and plastered onto the hooks. We lowered our armament into the quiet eddies behind rocks, then laid the poles flat in the gaps between the bridge floorboards and lay down ourselves as well, so we could peer down into that strange world through cupped hands.

Small fish materialized immediately. I can still see them, I think, hovering in quarrelsome bunches of three or five around each bait until the hungriest or the most foolish or the biggest or the littlest, overcome by the need to get it before its rivals did, screwed up its courage and rushed forward into oblivion. I don't remember what they were—a few were not trout certainly, for I do recall my uncle showing me a certain way to hold a fish, not more than six or eight inches long, so its stiff dorsal spines wouldn't harm me. Perch?

Each one went into the live bucket, then home and into the bathtub, of all things. My entrepreneurial uncle didn't have a paper route; he had a fish route. I remember only one of his accounts, the local parish priest, because of the dark and gloomy rectory we delivered our catch to. Vaguely, and finally, I remember a couple of domestic scenes involving our fish gasping on the floor in the bathroom, large puddles of water, and my grandmother, perhaps with hands on her hips .

The memory of this beginning has come to me twice most strongly: Once on my first visit—an adult now, or as close as I'll come—to Yellowstone Park, when I hung over Fishing Bridge with hundreds of other rubber-neckers to watch the opportunistic cutthroat trout snap up cigarette butts seemingly an arm's length away; and again a couple of years ago, as I waited for a floatplane on the dock of a lodge in the western Alaskan bush. I was sitting on a duffle, idly peering through the spaces between the boards into the clear river below. That and something else—could it have been a whiff of cheese from the lodge kitchen?—triggered a rush of *déjà vu* that almost spilled me over. It had the force of a sudden wave of tropical fever.

Maybe you can see that my life has become involved with fishing to an extent that no one could have guessed on that canton bridge. At every turn of my working life, when I made the choices that have led me here, the route seemed obvious; the path of least resistance. And at every new development in my "career," when others congratulated me or commented on my "job," I was able to keep a straight face and mumble something appropriate, while thinking gleefully, *"Sure beats working!"*

I can think of no other more common denominator for humankind—except maybe food or sex—than this fascination with peering into water to see what gives with the fish. Almost 32 million fishing licenses were sold in the U.S.A. last year, and that doesn't count the kids and saltwater fishermen who didn't need licenses. Sophisticated Swedish bankers do it. Mighty Japanese industrialists lose their cool completely over foot-long trout. A Bhutanese Buddhist monk, immersed in a centuries-old reverence for life, will struggle with his conscience only briefly before sidling over next to a Western angler to see how they're bitin'. Eskimos, Southern Baptists, Chinese peasants, Soviet apparatchiks and Wall Street traders all drop what they're doing at the chance to mess around with fish.

Analysts say they—we—are all transferring, seeking to trade places with wild, free things, to reduce our cares to their least state and restore harmony to our lives. Yes, certainly. And I say we all have some ancient memory of a bridge, or a farm pond, or a jetty, and the things that swam through the water to touch us.

Silvio Calabi
Camden, Maine

FRESHWATER
FISH

Bass

THE LARGE-MOUTHED BLACK BASS. (Micropterus Salmoides.)

THE LARGEMOUTH BASS has spawned, ahem, an industry. In fact the largemouth bass has *become* an industry. If there are truly sixty million sportfishermen in America, as estimated, then probably forty of those millions regard this largest of the sunfish family as numero uno on the hit parade. Bass fishing has become a sport unto itself, like trout fishing, but it's even more closely defined: For starters, there is only one largemouth bass (there are lots of different trout). And to "bass-fish" in the fullest sense one needs a large stable of advanced-composite-materials bassin' rods, each carrying an extraordinarily high-tech reel (with readouts for lure depth and speed); a kitchen-appliance-size tackle box of bass lures designed to swim, kick, pop, twist, gurgle and emit sexy scents at every level of the water column; an array of electronic water depth, temperature, pH and turbidity meters that would make a Soviet sub commander jealous; a bass boat (the performance of which is the envy of *any* navy and most drug runners) on which to stow all this gear, as well as food, beer, CB radio, stereo sound and the bass you do catch; a bass trailer; a bass four-wheel-drive; and a collection of jaunty bass caps and one-piece bass jumpsuits. The bass Winnebago is optional, as are the "kiss my bass" T-shirts and panties for your girlfriend. And then after you've learned to put this gear to the proper use, you may consider joining the bass tournament

A smallmouth bass warily holding its ground above the "structure" it calls home. Gilbert van Ryckevorsel photograph.

circuit, where the cash prizes are second only to pro golf and tennis.

The most interesting thing is that the largemouth just happens to be worth all this.

It possesses all the hallmarks of a great gamefish: a voracious appetite that regards everything from ducklings to its own offspring as table fare; a no-nonsense approach to feeding that often leaves the successful fisherman with cardiac palpitations; impressive strength and size; and a combination of low cunning and high intelligence that has proven the bass to be the smartest of our fish. Furthermore, thanks to stocking, largemouth bass are now found in every state, in all of Mexico and Central America, and throughout much of Canada and Europe.

Bass are warmwater fish. Although they thrive in the cool lakes of Michigan, Maine, Oregon and so on, they positively thrive in the warm, fecund waters of, say, Texas and Florida. Where there's lots of food year-round and where the more jungly landscape provides the kind of subsurface cover bass like to skulk around in. One of the bass fisherman's biggest challenges is to present his lures without hanging up on lily pads, water grasses, or drowned trees and brush. The next challenge is to provoke one of those heart-stopping strikes. Tests show the largemouth learns faster than other fish, and so grows jaded by baits and artificial lures. Once the fish recognizes everything you've got, sometimes the only solution is to find a new lure the fish hasn't yet seen. (Hence the van-sized tackle boxes.)

But you don't really need all the aforementioned materiel just to catch *a* bass (*the* bass, the local monster, perhaps so). Largemouth bass can be taken on all sorts of tackle, even streamer flies and flyrod poppers, and from canoes, float tubes and even from shore. It's just that catching one big, head-shaking, gill-rattling, bulldogging bass naturally makes you want to catch another, and another, and a bigger one. . . . Down that road lies the perfectly understandable bass madness that keeps tackle makers in business.

The largemouth bass, America's most popular gamefish. Minnesota Dept. of Natural Resources photograph.

An illustration of why the largemouth bass is familiarly known as both "bucketmouth" and "hawg"—and why it is such a popular gamefish. Scientific Anglers/3M photograph.

A cruising largemouth bass changes course to inspect the fisherman's bogus worm. Scientific Anglers/3M photograph.

The **smallmouth bass** is almost as popular, but maybe with a slightly different breed of angler—these fish live in deeper or cooler water, and often in rivers that may also be trout habitat. Smallmouths are smaller than largemouth bass (although the official world record of twelve-plus pounds would be respectable for a bigmouth too), a bit more streamlined, as befits fish that live in moving water, and often show indistinct dark vertical bars on their bronze-brown hide. The smallmouth naturally has a smaller mouth, too—the point of its jaw does not extend back past the eye, as on its larger cousin—so it isn't capable of swallowing the sort of prey that largemouth have built their reputation upon. But the smallmouth is a heavy feeder nonetheless, an ambusher of live food, and just as gamy an adversary on rod & line.

The scientists who proclaim the largemouth the smartest of our gamefish also rank the smallmouth highly. Only devoted smallmouth anglers disagree—they say their fish is much harder to fool consistently.

In a shallow, clear stream, you can sight-fish to a pair of these bass for a whole afternoon without a) spooking them or b) catching one. But that's no reason not to try: Start right at the tail of a pool, where the constricted flow and greater current concentrate the food passing by. If a baitfish lure doesn't bring a strike, consider switching to fly tackle and seductively twitching a feathery leech pattern through the same water, down near the bottom. Failing that, a couple of box-stock trout flies, such as a little nymph or even a generic dry fly, may bring a strike. If the fish have seen all this before, it may be time for the closest thing to a sure-fire smallmouth "gitter"—live bait, in the form of a crayfish lightly hooked through the tail. Your target fish may fall upon this offering with the equivalent of glad cries, interrupting only to bash each other away from your hook. It's almost sad to see such smart alecks turn instantly into gibbering idiots.

After these two black basses, the handsome **crappie**—pronounced "croppie"—is the next largest of the sunfish (probably in popularity as well as in size). Crappies come in black and white varieties—the former often preferring cooler, deeper, sometimes moving water, the latter more a southern shallows-dweller, but there is plenty of crossover.

Crappie grow sometimes as large as four pounds, with the distinctive pear-shaped bodies of "sunnies." Their most unusual feature is their fins: Both anal and dorsal fins are very similar in size and shape (like long, graceful Japanese fans) and are located almost directly one above the other, just aft of the midline of the body. Few freshwater fish show such bilateral symmetry, so crappies are easy to identify in general. It's telling the black from the white that's harder, as they are commonly the same color—dark green/olive/black backs above silvery sides. And both are heavily spotted. But the spots on the white crappie are arranged more or less into irregular vertical bars, while the black crappie's spots are sprinkled on haphazardly. And scientists say the black crappie has seven or eight spines in its dorsal fin while the white has no more than six.

Crappies are often uninterested in surface feeding, so the angler should go down to them. These quick-striking fish fall for a great variety of lures—everything from live minnows to small spinners and spoons to flyrod streamers. They congregate in large schools and, like all sunfish, are particularly susceptible in defense of their spring spawning grounds. (You may in fact be reminded of the old saw about shooting fish in a barrel.) Reportedly, when biologist Elgin Ciampi tested eight fish species for intelligence, the crappie scored a lowly seventh—ahead of only the gar—in learning to avoid lures. Once you've located a school, the most difficult aspect of boating crappies may be hanging onto them—their mouth tissue is very fragile and hooks tear out easily. But if you use a net you'll soon be in good shape for a fish fry.

A predatory largemouth accelerates forward to inhale a small sunfish, which is stiffening its dorsal spines in a vain attempt to discourage the attack. Scientific Anglers/3M photograph.

THE SMALL-MOUTHED BLACK BASS.(Micropterus dolomieu.)

Catfish

THE BULLHEAD
(Amiurus nebulosus)

THE SERIOUS CATFISHERMAN is a breed apart, something of a rarity among us sporting types. The catfish, in all its species, is different too, at least among the fish in this book; it is a bottom feeder. The catfish's appearance is unique also, among gamefish: snaky barbels, which are in fact sensitive organs of touch/ smell that let the fish prosper in low visibility, sprout from its mouth and chin like the mustachios of a comic-book villain. The mouth is flat and wide, like a rubbery gash across its flat and even wider shovel-shaped head. The eyes appear piggy and small. Its slaty gray-brown or blue-black hide bears no scales at all, and reflects little light. None of the coruscating beauty of a brook trout here. This is obviously a creature of the deep, and men who would have it must go there in pursuit; the catfish won't be lured upward.

There are two reasons for wanting to do this. First, inevitably, the challenge: A big catfish—some get *very* big—is a tough customer. And second, catfish, and their close relatives the hornpout, are superb table fare, so much so that they have

been a major aquacultural crop in the South for decades. Despite their looks, catfish are not garbage feeders, and your first taste of catfish fry will confirm this—like us, catfish are what they eat, and they are delicious.

But back to the challenge. The big-water **blue catfish** is the largest prize. Specimens approaching 120 pounds have been hoisted (on very heavy gear) from deep, swift Mississippi River tailwaters, and 200-pounders were reportedly taken in Civil War times. In the right places today, thirty-pounders are almost everyday catches. Blues can be awesome predators, feeding on other fish and crayfish, and are usually caught on natural baits that would astonish most freshwater fishermen—whole large suckers, for instance. **Channel catfish** also like deep water and clean bottoms, in larger rivers and lakes. Channel cats have deeply forked tails, are often spotted, and are maybe "sportier" than blues—they will often strike artificial lures like deep-running spoons. Although they grow to fifty pounds or so, five- to ten-pound channel cats are impressive gamefish. They too are voracious predators and, with generally sleeker bodies than other catfish, fast swimmers that sometimes enter small streams to spawn.

(They seem to tolerate colder water too: Around 1980, a boy fishing for trout hooked and landed what proved to be a tremendous channel cat—in a Vermont stream. The uproar among local fly fishermen was spectacular, but eventually died down when it became clear that the trout were not being decimated and that there were no more big cats. One theory is that the fish was planted, as a prank, by someone visiting the area in a motorhome.)

The olive-drab **flathead** is the third of North America's giant catfish, and it too is most plentiful in the Mississippi corridor. It's easy to distinguish because it is the only cat with a rounded, blunt tail, like a hornpout's, while its size and distinctively disagreeable looks (it is appropriately named) set it well apart from the 'pouts too. A big one goes about a hundred pounds and maybe sixteen inches between the eyes, but ten pounds is normal. Flatheads—sometimes known as mudcats—are pure predators, and they can be found in shallow water,

lurking in ambush in their riverbank lairs like pike. Thus the "sport" of noodling for flatheads: A fisherman cautiously wades to the den, eases his arm into the dark water, and ever so slowly feels around until he can suddenly thrust his hand into the fish's gaping mouth, grab a gill, and heave the monster onto the bank. Fun, eh? You might well wonder who caught whom. Tales of noodlers who were themselves dragged kicking and screaming underwater abound in catfish country.

Specialists who go after big cats have many methods to choose from, but if you leave off nets, traps and the like and concentrate on hook & line, the basics involve a huge sinker, to hold the offering on the bottom in heavy current, and, tied into the line above, one or more huge hooks baited with something revolting. As in chicken guts, smelly cheese, oil-soaked sponges, doughballs,

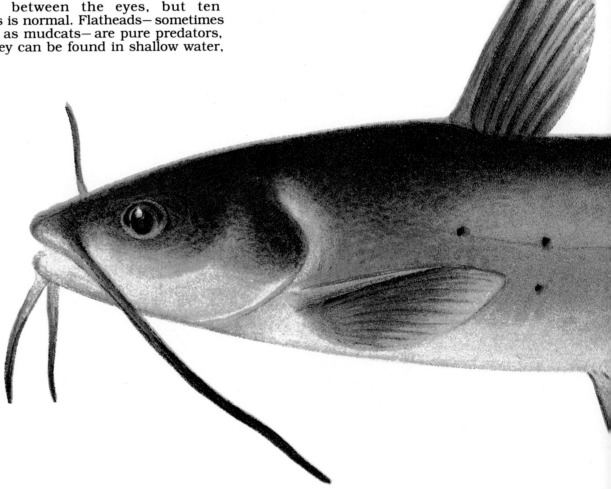

SPOTTED CATFISH (ICTALURUS PUNCTA

frogs and whole or sectioned fish. Catfish baits needn't even be edible, at least by human standards; there is a school of catfishermen who rely on different brands of soap for bait. At the other end of the line there's usually some sort of stout float—anything from commercial plastic bobbers to milk jugs. Catfish are nocturnal feeders, and perhaps you can imagine the pandemonium caused by a hookup with a huge fish in the dark, on a heavy flowing, tricky river.

There's one more important American cat, the comparatively small and meek **white catfish** that lives on the East and West coasts and in Great Lakes rivers. The recorded world record is a mere seventeen and a half pounds, and a ten-pounder is rare. But whites are top panfish also, and kids from Maine to Michigan to California have learned to catch them on pint-sized versions of the tackle used in the Midwest.

Hornpout—or maybe horned pout, or bullpout, or bullheads—are members of the catfish family distinguished by their small size and rounded tails. One or another of the 'pout species (brown, black, yellow, flathead, etc.) are found in almost every part of America, and annually millions of them find their way into skillets and freezers.

While a big river cat is pounds and pounds of moist, succulent white meat, a little bullhead, undressed for the pan, is often pinkish, equally tasty, and sized and shaped like an ear of corn. And, after deep-frying, that's just how you eat them.

One of my earliest memories of fishing is watching the neighborhood nannies and cleaning ladies catch hornpout in the evenings, grouped companionably together on folding chairs on the beach of a tiny lake in the town where I grew up. The fish never seemed to die, thrashing in the pails no matter how long the owner stayed at the lake. (When I grew older and could catch them for myself, I discovered that, eerily, they truly never did seem to die, or at least they never stopped squirming, even after being gutted and skinned!)

Hornpout are as important to an American childhood as sunfish. They are easy to catch—just heave out a hook decorated with worms or a bit of leftover school lunch; abundant almost everywhere there are muddy ponds; and ugly and just dangerous enough, thanks to that sharp spine on the fins that can inflict a painful stab, to thrill kids deeply. Now that I think about it, how come more of us don't graduate from bullheads to full emotional involvement with catfish?

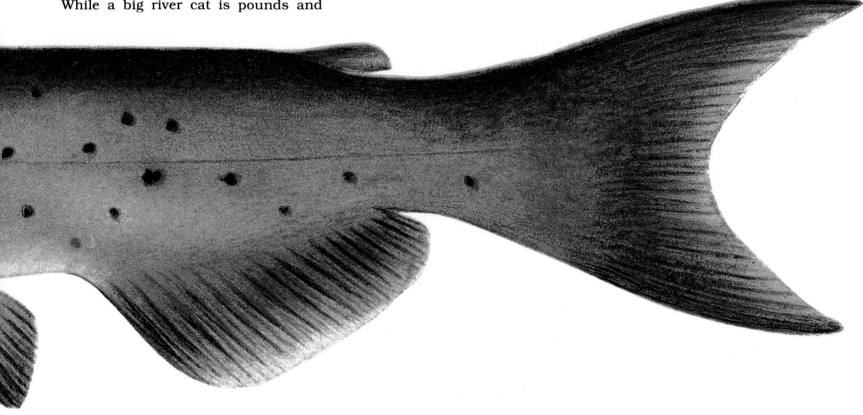

JS (RAFINESQUE)]

A tackle-caught channel catfish, showing net marks on its smooth sides and destined for the table. Don Blegen photograph.

A small blue catfish investigates the lake bottom with its sensitive barbels. Minnesota Dept. of Natural Resources photograph.

Grayling

THE GRAYLING is a trickster among North American gamefish. The bigger ones, that hide in deep pools and runs, strike a hook and fight like Dolly Varden or even small salmon. But the little fellows, the ones that pop up in the riffles or in calm, sun-warmed shallows, dimple the surface like panfish. The grayling is a puzzle in other ways too— in unfished wilderness waters they can become stubbornly selective, while at other times it seems a bit of parka lining on a hook will attract a mob. It's a shame more fishermen don't get to see them, but they're a northern fish, found in great numbers only in Alaska and north-western Canada. Remnant populations exist down into the American Rockies, and a century ago they were so populous in the upper Midwest as to be commercial market fish.

In spite of this rarity, everyone knows the grayling— it's that pretty little number with the iridescent purplish-greenish-silvery hide and the huge dorsal fin. It's probably this fancy dress, and the fact that they live in sportfishing country, that elevates grayling to the ranks of great gamefish, for they are not spectacular fighters. (After all, how much tussle can you expect from a fish that tops out at two or three pounds?) Grayling can be caught on flies, lures and bait with equal success. Many Alaskan anglers look to the grayling for rest from the salmon and trout battles; after days of slugging it out with heavy tackle in big water, it can be a welcome change to pick up ultralight tackle and stalk active, surface-feeding two-pound grayling. They are excellent table fare, too; stranded in the Cassiar Mountains of northern British Columbia, four of us ate grayling for two weeks straight and never tired of that firm, delicate white meat.

Interested in an IGFA world record? The streams of the west-central coast of Alaska shelter the biggest grayling I've seen anywhere. I released one of twenty-four inches there in the summer of '86, and plenty only a little smaller.

Its showy dorsal fin distinguishes the arctic grayling. This large specimen was taken in British Columbia by the photographer, David Lambroughton.

Panfish

IT'S AN UGLY WORD, but it's going to stick around, even among the millions of fishermen who prefer *not* to pop them into a skillet at day's end: panfish. The angling equivalent of "small game." Sure, it's hard to strike a heroic pose with a stringer of shellcrackers, just like a beltfull of squirrels isn't quite the same as an eight-point whitetail. But that shouldn't relegate panfish to second-class-fish status. While they are certainly not big-game fish, and you may not regard them as gamefish, no one can dispute that they are game fish, if you see what I mean.

These fish are game as can be, in fact—quick as rattlesnakes to defend their mate and nest, pugnacious fighters on hook & line, strong and handsome and even plentiful. Although the word panfish can be applied to hornpout, yellow perch, crappie and other species, I'm talking about the smaller sunfishes, such as the **bluegill**.

If bluegill grew to the size of, say, Frisbees, no one would pay attention to permit any more; they would simply have been upstaged as one of earth's hardest-fighting fish. The bluegill's broad, flat sides give it tremendous "traction" in the water, and when you back that kind of leverage up with the muscle and disposition of a predator, you have a gutsy opponent that can make your line sing as it cuts doughnuts through the water. But bluegills rarely grow larger than eight or ten inches, and, as they often live cheek-by-gills with largemouth bass, many fall for bass gear that is just too heavy for proper sport.

But arm yourself with wispy tackle and stalk the bluegill and its many cousins on purpose. They'll go for almost anything—tiny spinners and spoons, all manner of cheese, worms and other bait, maybe even a scrap of your T-shirt on a weighted hook. But truly the best way to fish for them is with a fly rod. Not a designer bamboo mounted with an English reel (well, then again, . . .) but a floppy old glass rod and your uncle's hand-me-down automatic, and a handful of rubber-legged, horribly colored little

A happy fisherman with the makings of a crappie bake for the whole neighborhood. He uses the long pole to reach deep into brushy pockets where the fish feel protected. William Greer photograph.

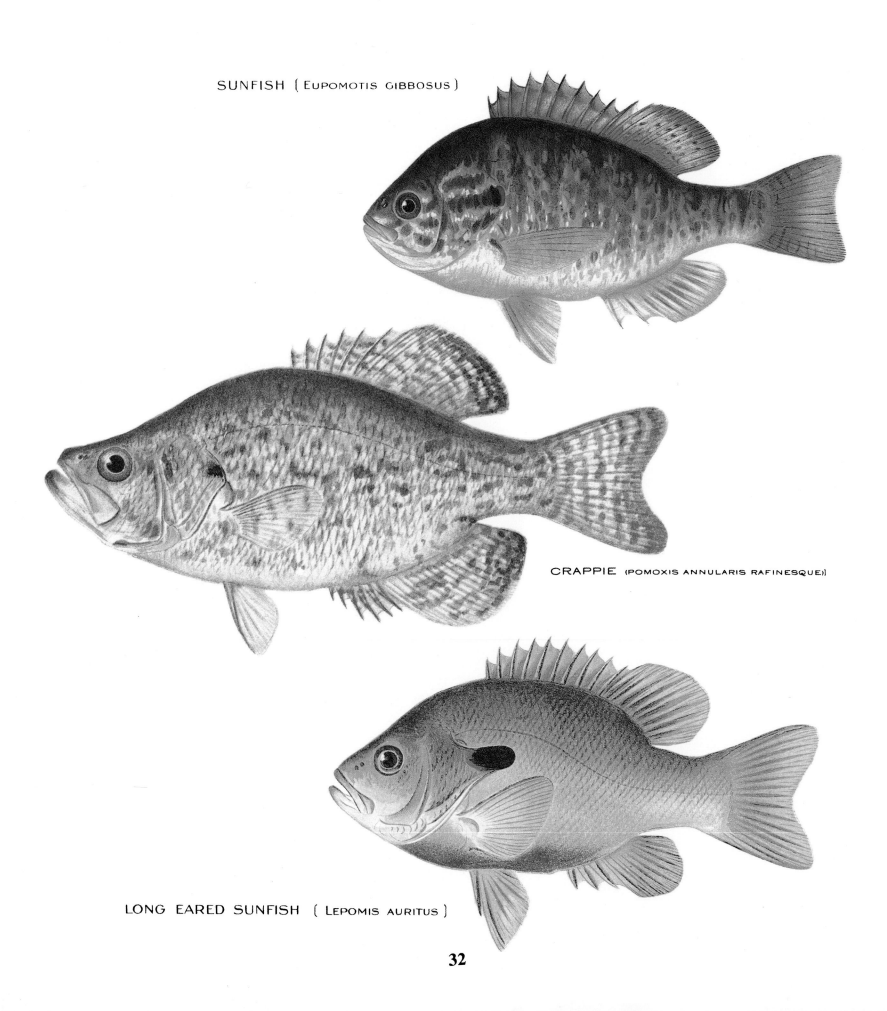

SUNFISH (Eupomotis gibbosus)

CRAPPIE (pomoxis annularis rafinesque)]

LONG EARED SUNFISH (Lepomis auritus)

32

topwater poppers. There's no need here for the far-and-fine fly presentation of the trout angler; just plop that thing down in the warm summer shallows near a weed bed and twitch it a bit.

A bluegill strikes a popper with pursed lips that make a distinctive kissing noise as they break the surface. On a still day, in clear water, it's fascinating to watch blugills hover underneath, inspecting the fly, then dart upward to smack it. It's the best way I know to learn to handle fly tackle and have fun at the same time.

Bluegills have, uh, blue gills. That is, the little "ear" flap at the rear of their gill covers is deep blue or even black and lacks the contrasting red-orange spot typical of most sunfish. The **pumpkinseed** has it, but it almost disappears in this fish's brilliant coloring, which runs to green-blue stripes radiating across its orange head and stomach, and olive green back and sides shot through with more orange or yellow. The **red-ear sunfish**, widely known in its native South as the shellcracker, for the teeth with which it grinds up snails, looks much like a toned-down pumpkinseed but has a distinctive red edge to its gill flap and no bands across its head. Red-ears grow to an impressive three pounds-plus, eating almost anything and everything— in some Alabama lakes, for example, they feed heavily at the surface on willowfly hatches, just like trout. There's also a **redbreast** sunfish, which look like it should be a bluegill-pumpkinseed cross but isn't, that lives in East-Coast smallmouth rivers; a **green** sunfish that is almost as streamlined as a bass; the tiny **longear** sunfish, which prefers cooler and often flowing water; **spotted** sunfish; and a host of hybrids that only add to the fishing— and the confusion.

A redbreast sunfish, photographed by Joel Arrington.

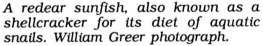

A redear sunfish, also known as a shellcracker for its diet of aquatic snails. William Greer photograph.

A school of bluegill sunfish. Minnesota Dept. of Natural Resources photograph.

Perch

THE PIKE PERCH OR WALL-EYED PIKE (Stizostedium Vitreum)

RIGHT UP THERE alongside the large-mouth bass and the entire trout family in popularity with American fishermen is the homely **walleye**. For a fish to be so well-known and loved, it must be wide-ranging—which it is, occurring naturally and through stocking in Canada and all but the Gulf Coast states—and it must have some outstanding attributes as a gamefish. The walleye is not a water-thrashing, tackle-tearing fighter. Nor is it so beautiful an animal that we seek it out just to photograph it or mount it. But it *is* 1) fairly easy to catch, 2) ugly enough that no one seems to mind knocking it over the head, and 3) very tasty.

The walleye's wide range is why it has so many—dozens, in fact—local names. It's not a pike, despite its teeth and predatory habits; rather it is the largest member of the perch family, with the characteristic second dorsal fin. (The current IGFA record is a twenty-five pounder caught in 1960 in Tennessee.) Anyone who has ever seen a walleye understands the name immediately—its eyes do in fact look helplessly blind and opaque. The opposite is true, though, particularly at night, when those big eyes become a huge advantage in feeding. Ironically, they help fishermen locate them as well, for they reflect light noticeably, even underwater.

Look for walleyes near the bottom of fairly clean, fairly cool waters—lakes and slower-moving rivers. Many successful fishermen slowly troll baitfish imitations along the drop-offs from shallow to deep water. When the first walleye hits, they anchor to still-fish, for they know that these fish often congregate in large schools.

The walleye's humble relative, the **yellow perch**, is a member of that loose category known as panfish. And appropriately, like the walleye perch, the yellow variety is worth popping into a pan. (Certainly it is on no one's endangered-species list—it's one of the few gamefish that shows up in probably every state.) Its meat is white, delicate and in enough demand that there is a substantial commercial fishery for perch in the Great Lakes.

A brightly colored yellow perch that fell victim to a rubber-legged "slider" fly. Joel Arrington photograph.

Like the pike and the striped bass, the yellow perch is one of the most easily recognized fish, thanks to the half-dozen or more vertical dark bars that pepper its yellowish body, and the twin dorsal fins. Perch strike lures, flies and bait pretty much all year round—in fact, they are a popular target of ice-fishermen. While boatloads of us adults secretly get a kick out of perch, I suspect their greatest value is to kids. I know full well that I wouldn't be writing this today if it hadn't been for the hundreds of scrappy little perch that obligingly sunk my bobbers thirty and more years ago.

A bragging-size walleye—not a pike but a perch. Jim Lindner, The In-Fisherman, photograph.

Pikes

The northern pike normally waits in ambush for foodfish, then strikes and withdraws in an eyeblink, its prey often clamped crosswise in its jaws the way a dog carries a bone. Bill Roston photograph.

THE NORTHERN PIKE has about the same appeal to fishermen as the wolf or the grizzly does to some big-game hunters. But while the rapacious nature of the two animals is grossly exaggerated, old *Esox lucius*, the waterwolf, is indeed a nasty customer— at least to foodfish, ducklings and the odd baby muskrat. The name itself comes from the fish's resemblance to the slim and deadly blade of that favorite medieval weapon. Early angling literature has many pike stories, mostly about monsters of dubious authenticity that would outstrip even world-class barracuda. However, the biggest pike still occur in northern Europe, where fifty-pounders are reported almost every year, and there are reasonably credible tales of seventy-pound Amur pike in Mongolia. So perhaps some of the legendary Irish and German monsters did exist. Few North American northerns exceed twenty-five pounds (despite Alaskan tales of giant "jackfish" that swallow canoes), but given the pike's long, slim body, such a fish makes a very respectable showing in a net. Originally found only north of about 60 degrees latitude, pike made their way into New England more than a century ago, and have since been transplanted throughout

MASKALONGE [LUCIUS OHIENSIS (KIRTLAND)]

THE PIKE. (LUCIUS LUCIUS. L.)

THE PICKEREL. (LUCIUS RETICULATUS. LE SUEUR.)
FROM A POND IN MASSACHUSETTS.

A northern pike, the "waterwolf," turns to inspect the camera. Minnesota Dept. of Natural resources photograph.

the Midwest and as far south as North Carolina.

(By contrast, the pike's smaller cousin, the chain pickerel, also an *Esox*, occurs naturally almost everywhere east of the Mississippi drainage. Too small to be considered "real" gamefish, the pickerel and its slashing strike has nevertheless hooked millions of kids on a lifetime of fishing.)

Pike like fairly still, fairly shallow water, often lying in motionless ambush under some sort of cover, waiting like a mugger for a little old lady with her Welfare. There are exceptions, as always. While wading a swift Labrador river, I almost stepped on a medium-sized pike that was lying in six inches of water in the lee of a rock; it had a ten-inch brook trout sideways in its jaws. The pike rolled one eye upward, studied me, then deliberately swallowed the trout down before shooting away into the current.

The way to take pike is by playing their game— swimming a baitfish imitation low and slow past their noses, or attracting them to the surface with a noisy top-water lure. They are sprinters; a pike will dash from its lie, clamp down on its target, and stop. Your lure will too. When you lean on the fish, what happens next depends on how big it is, but in any case the next few minutes can be spectacular. I've never seen pike jump, except on the strike (one launched itself right out of the water into a shallow racing dive in its hurry to fall on my "escaping" popper), but they'll try everything else. And they are tenacious: Several times I've boated pike that weren't even hooked— they had the fly in a deathgrip and just wouldn't let go. Pike teeth will tear up terminal tackle (and your fingers, if you're careless in unhooking them) in a hurry; the trick is to use long-bodied flies or lures, steel swivels and/or wire or heavy mono-filament shock tippets. And check your tackle after every strike.

There is another way to take pike, legal in very few places— by shooting them. In Vermont, for example, there's a ten-day spring season; northerns by the thousands spawn in the flooded shores of Lake Champlain, and a few diehard locals hunt them from canoes or on foot, in waders, bearing heavy-caliber handguns or shotguns loaded with slugs.

A spawning pike, especially a large female, is easily spotted by her dorsal fin sticking out of the water. As the pike's fin is very close to the tail, it takes keen judgement and a good eye to put a round into the muddy water next to the unseen head. The concussion kills or stuns the fish, which then floats belly-up. Pike taken this way are often smoked, which dissolves a number of the pesky little bones, and are delicious. A most bizarre and occasionally dangerous sport that, in the spooky, flooded forest, sometimes takes on the aspect of a jungle firefight.

There are still places where fishermen "release" pike by batting them across the water with canoe paddles, but in this day and age most of us recognize that predators, be they wolves or pike, are just as important as prey to the balance of nature. Live and let live goes for pike as well as for trout and salmon.

If you're after American "pike" of legendary old-world proportions, the **muskellunge** is your fish. Like all good monsters, it is fairly rare and has a restricted northeastern/upper midwestern range (helps build up the stories, you see), and it's, well, big. The IGFA recognizes a 70-pound musky caught in 1957 in New York's St. Lawrence River as the all-tackle record, but as always bigger, if unverified, specimens have been taken. For all intents and purposes, consider the musky an even-larger version of the northern pike, with dark markings—bars or spots—against a light body color, whereas the pike bears light oblong patches on a darker background. And where pike and pickerel have scales all over their cheeks (forward of the gill covers), the muskellunge's cheeks have scales only on the upper half, if at all. Fish-story-wise, take everything you've heard or seen about northern pike, magnify it, and you'll be prepared for muskies: If a pike could take your finger off, a musky could do your hand, and so on.

Fishing for muskies gets into people's blood. The musky's size—only king salmon, sturgeon and a few catfish are larger, in fresh water—and scarcity—Canadian biologists say that experienced musky fishermen average one hundred angling hours per legal fish—and dining habits—anything up to small beavers is fair game—put it in a class by itself. Musky fishermen call their sport a cat-and-mouse game, with man as the mouse.

Muskellunge have been caught on flies, but the experts use heavy baitcasting tackle rigged with huge topwater plugs. Because big muskies seem rare even in good water, locating their lies is as important as it is to the trophy brown-trout fisherman. (I say the fish *seem* rare, but what I mean is that hookups are rare; no one knows how many lures a big old musky ignores before finally lunging after one.) Working shallow, weedy shorelines, drop your plug into the water so that it seems to be struggling toward the safety of land or cover, and then crank it on home. Give it lots of life by jigging your rod tip and varying the retrieve speed. Don't let it stop long enough for Mr. Musky to get a good look at it; let him see only action—bubbles, blurs, drunken dives and staggers. The fish may follow you right to the boat before striking, or it may not strike at all, just hanging momentarily in the water a rod length away before vanishing from sight.

Stunning as this can be, the most overcome is usually the bass or panfish angler who unwittingly drops his lure on top of a hungry musky. To be suddenly attacked by something roughly the size, shape, disposition and speed of a cruise missile can provoke cardiac stutters.

Although there are many local names for this gamefish, science recognizes only one species, the muskellunge, and one variant, the **tiger musky**. This strikingly striped predator is a hybrid, the offspring of a northern pike and a muskellunge, and is considered the catch of a lifetime by many fishermen. Like a mule, the tiger musky is sterile. So if by some fantastic stroke of luck you hook and boat a tiger approaching the all-tackle record of 51 pounds 3 ounces, by all means knock it on the head and have it mounted, for it can't make little tigers even if you do let it go.

A very fine specimen of Canadian northern pike. Jim Lardner, The In-Fisherman, photograph.

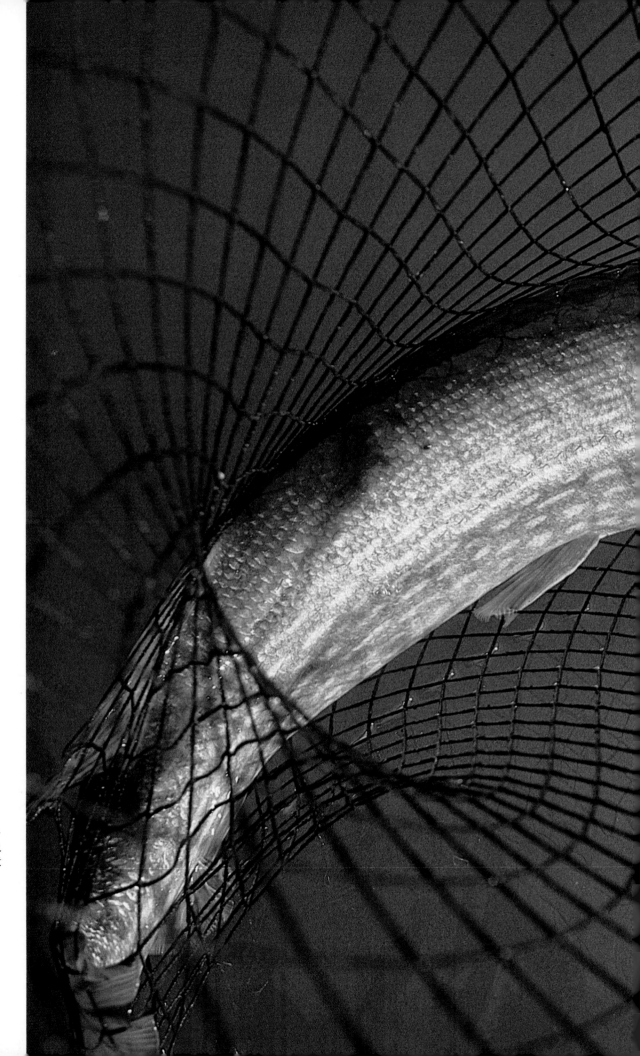

It takes a large net to swallow twenty-five pounds of northern pike. The fish is still chewing the tinsel fly that fooled it. Author's photograph.

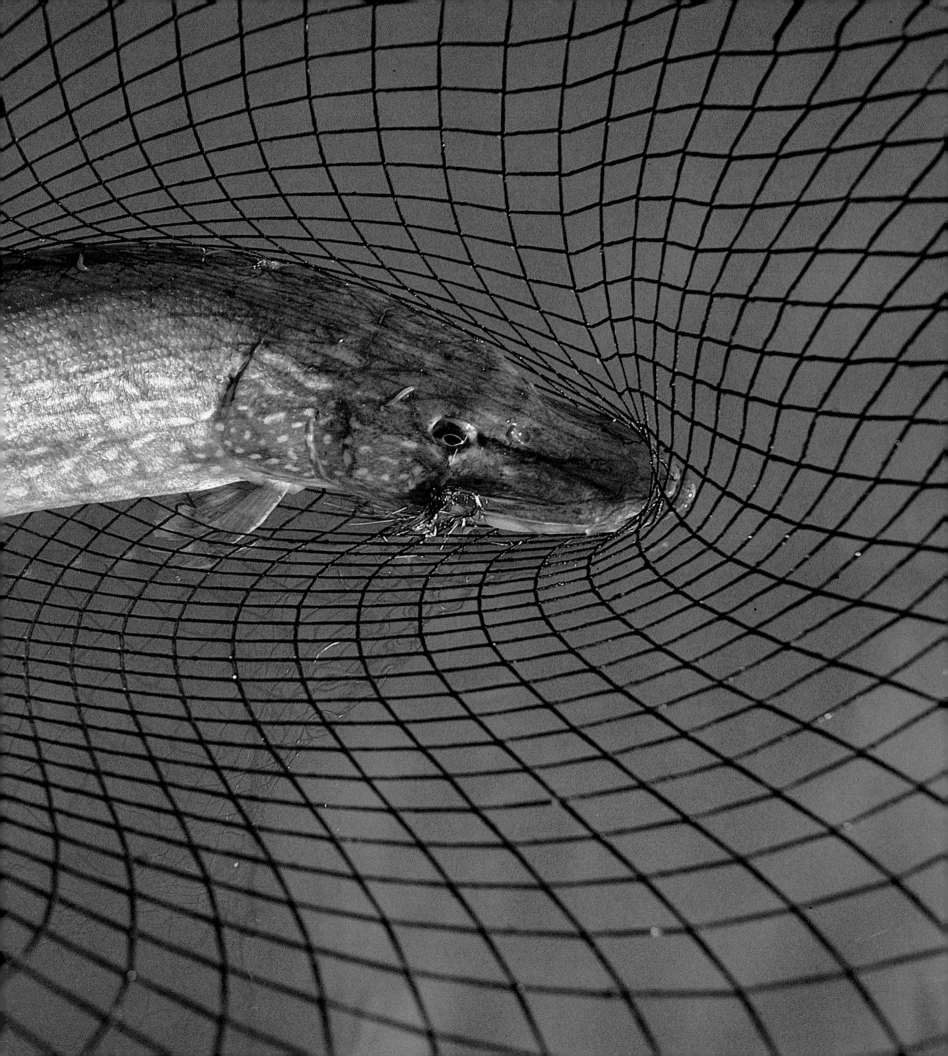

Sea-RunFish

Salmo salar, the Atlantic salmon. Author's photograph.

THE SALMON, an anadromous fish, has grown up at sea, feeding upon seemingly limitless shoals of herring, small crabs, squid, and plankton such as krill and shrimp. Barring encounters with commercial fishermen and a few other predators, life is grand out in the open ocean—there's room to roam, and little to cramp this fish's bold style. But in two or three years, or five or more in some individuals, an age-old hunger draws the salmon out of the infinite, safe deeps and launches them upon a journey few will survive. The need to spawn, to reproduce the species, to keep the eternal cycle going, urges the salmon toward shore to find their home river.

Relying on a sense of smell/taste far keener than any scientific instrument yet built by man, salmon home in on minute traces of fresh river water mingling with the sea. As they enter the estuaries they swam out of several years earlier as young smolts, their troubles begin. As the coast begins to embrace the salmon within its headlands, the seals increase. Fishing boats find them easily and corner the schools with their nets. In the rivermouths the bottom shoals rapidly and even hungry seabirds

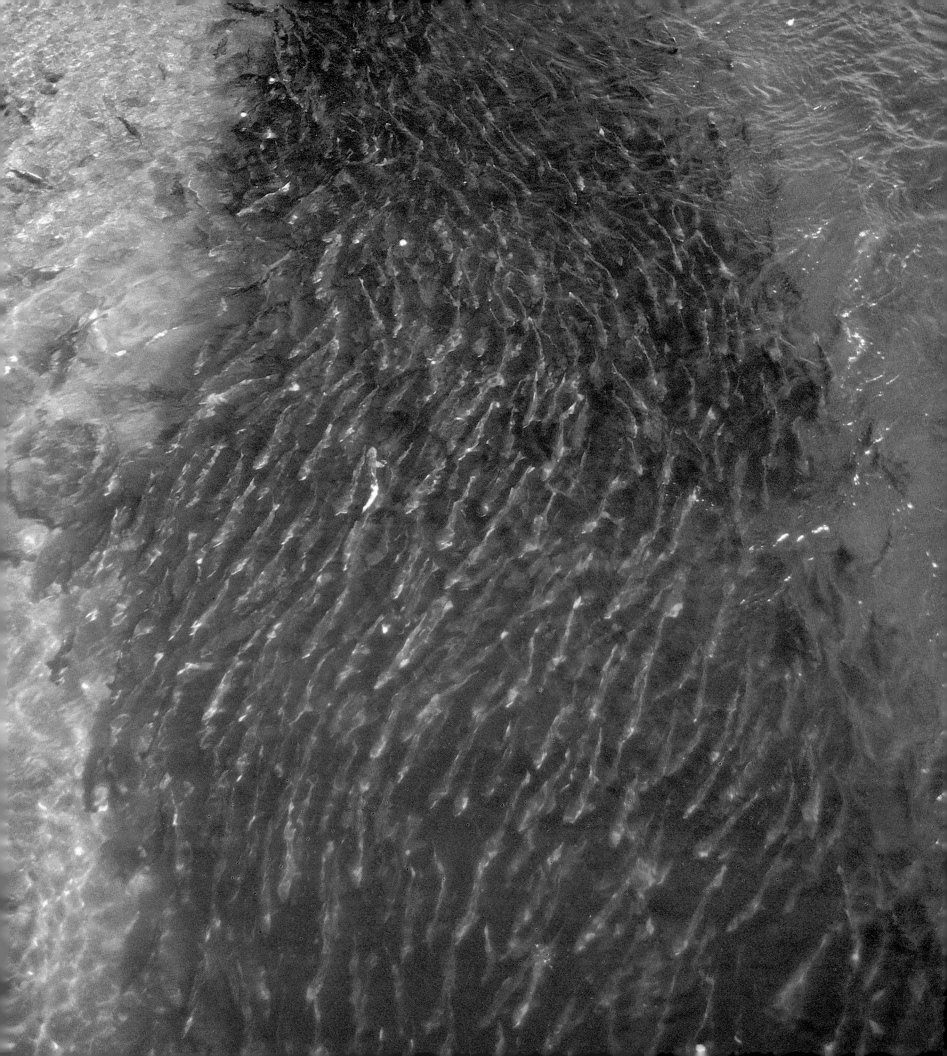

Preceding page:
A spectacular "run" of Alaskan sockeye salmon, migrating upstream to spawn in late summer. David Lambroughton photograph.

A prime, bright-silver coho salmon fresh from the Pacific Ocean and about to be released back into its spawning river. David Lambroughton photograph.

Atlantic salmon resting deep in a pool on their way up Quebec's Grand Cascapedia River to spawn. Gilbert van Ryckevorsel photograph.

can now reach the fish. The salmon that survive pass up into the still-narrower confines of their streams and rivers, and the predation begins in earnest.

Otters, mink, fisher cats, ospreys and eagles. In the far Northwest, the great brown bears have been waiting since they emerged from their winter dens for the salmon to appear. And man is there too—man the netter, man the poacher, and man the angler.

Little wonder then that the salmon—grown outlandishly strong in the wide sea, now hemmed in by streambanks, forced to combat swift river currents, unable to eat, and diverted from the spawning imperative by predators of every sort—becomes a tiger on rod and line, a champion battler for freedom. A freshwater gamefish without superior and with few equals.

Along the Northeastern coast, from the Connecticut River and along the St. Lawrence to the northern capes of New-foundland and Ungava Bay, the returning fish are **Atlantic salmon**. Here sportsmen may take them only by fly-fishing, a tradition that harkens back more than a century to the beginnings of salmon sportfishing in Britain. An Atlantic salmon is at least three years old, perhaps six or in rare cases seven years old when it first returns to fresh water in late spring and summer. It may be as small as ten pounds or as large as forty or more pounds, depending on genetic traits and time and conditions at sea. Upon entering its river, each salmon is shiny bright, carrying perhaps a sprinkling of irregular black markings on its sides and darker back. If sea lice are still attached to the fish, it has been out of salt water only a few hours.

The salmon have returned to spawn, and *only* to spawn. They will not, and cannot, eat at all; their metabolisms have changed, diverting energy from the digestive organs to the sexual organs.

This then is the eternal question facing the salmon fisherman: How to lure a fish that won't eat to a "baited" hook? Theories are that salmon strike a fly out of curiosity; out of aggession, to defend themselves or their mate or their nest; or through a conditioned response, an instinctive surrender to a sequence of events that a month earlier meant food. No matter the why, the most successful salmon anglers are those who have learned a river well enough to pinpoint, even in high, dark water, the lies where the migrating fish rest—the rocks, snags, ledges and shelves of the river bottom itself that break the current. Salmon consistently

hole up in the same spots on their way upstream, and a fly swum just so through their "window" of visibility will bring a strike.

Or it may not. Like everyone who's fished for salmon, I've spent hours and even days casting long to holding fish: I can see the torpedo shapes in the water when the light is right, but I know they're there also because often, as if to egg me on, a fish rolls mightily on the surface, which makes my knees turn to sponge rubber. All ignore my fly no matter how many times I change pattern, size and the depth and speed at which the fly swims. Then, when my patience is gone and frustration gets the upper hand, I fling out one more last cast and rip it back through the water, my mind already on home or the next pool. Sure enough—out of the corner of my eye I see a swirl, a broad back rise through the surface, then feel a solid bump on my line—but that's all, because I was mentally gone, my concentration broken. Stupid SOB! Won't I ever learn?

As water flow and temperatures permit, small bands of salmon struggle "home," sometimes winning their way a hundred miles or more upstream until they reach a pool with the right combination of current and substrate. The hen fish selects a spot and, holding herself almost flat to the bottom, sends the gravel flying with powerful strokes of her broad tail. With the aid of the current she soon has scoured out a large, shallow redd, or nest, in which she deposits her eggs. The male fish takes his turn, fertilizing the eggs with a cloud of milt, and then the hen goes back to work, covering the eggs with new gravel she digs from just upstream. In so doing, she creates another redd and often uses that as well, eventually laying some 7,000 to 20,000 eggs.

The fingerlings hatch soon and like their parents they overwinter in the river. The mature fish that have survived these months in fresh water—still without feeding—are called kelts, or black salmon, and they are pitifully thin and dark. Still facing upriver as though heeding the echo of the spawning urge, they allow the spring currents to push them back to the sea, where a fortunate few feed and grow and regain their strength for another run. The salmon young, first called parr, pass their first two or three years in the river until, as smolts of maybe eight inches, they too head for the salt.

Estimates are that maybe only ten percent of Atlantic salmon survive to spawn a second time. A very few ac-

A pair of grilse, small Atlantic salmon, legally killed for the smokehouse. Author's photograph.

complish this three and perhaps even four times.

Thanks to restrictions on commercial netters, North American salmon populations have rebounded somewhat in the last decade. Efforts are under way also to transplant Atlantics into some Great Lakes streams, and much time and money is being spent on restoring the salmon rivers of New England, with growing success. The catch in Maine's Penobscot River (in pools in downtown Bangor!) approaches a thousand fish every year. Canadian Atlantic salmon fishing is still often regarded as a blue-blood sport, but as the fishing improves the many miles of public water do too. Some of the best salmon water in the world is now available to anyone with a week's vacation, a car and enough cash to swing a few days' camping. As the emphasis swings away from private water, and as new catch-and-release

regulations take effect, a new breed of salmon angler is developing—younger, more conservation-minded, more attuned to current trends in angling.

Lee Wulff, the greatest American salmon angler, likens the fish in fresh water to an electric battery. Charged with energy from its seasons at sea, it must survive without food for almost a year. The angler who hooks one, plays it and releases it has drawn down that charge, forced the fish to spend some of its vital strength. And so it is doubly important that the fisherman play the salmon well, to avoid injuring it directly (by hooking it elsewhere than in the mouth or by dragging it onto sand or rocks to land it) and to avoid playing it too long. Many fishermen now use special leaders between fly and line that let them break off a salmon that can't be landed within an acceptably short time span. A good gamefish, said Lee Wulff

many years ago, is too valuable to be caught only once.

The **landlocked salmon** is about identical to the Atlantic salmon; it's simply not able to go to sea because of physical barriers—a dam, for example, either natural or manmade. Therefore it substitutes a deep, clear, cold lake for the ocean in which to mature, and then in the fall the landlock swims up into a tributary stream or river to go through the same spawning ritual.

It is now known that after the most recent glaciation, which withdrew from New England about 10,000 years ago, large populations of such freshwater salmon were established in Labrador, Newfoundland, and New Brunswick and Quebec, and as far inland as Lake Ontario. However, overfishing, pollution, dams and habitat destruction shrank the range of the landlocked to Maine and to eastern Canada, where the fish is called

the *ouananiche*.

Recognizing the value of this somewhat unique gamefish, the state of Maine has been researching landlocked-salmon biology since 1868. And with some success, too: Maine salmon eggs and fry have to date been transplanted to the waters of some two dozen other states and foreign countries, and now landlocks are once again found throughout the Northeast into Michigan.

Bowing to scientific evidence, the IGFA (the International Game Fish Association, which keeps modern sportfishing records) not long ago did away with the separate category for landlocked salmon in its record books, combining it instead with its near-twin, the Atlantic salmon. Because the sea-run variety is inevitably larger, this meant that the grand twenty-two-plus-pound landlocked caught in Maine's Sebago Lake in 1907 was disqualified as a

An Alaskan chum, or dog, salmon—so-called because the native people netted them to feed to their sled dogs over the winters—beginning to turn spawning red. Author's photograph.

salmon record. To the thousands of passionate landlocked fishermen of New England, this was a blow to their pride—henceforth they would have to regard their premier gamefish as nothing more than a scaled-down Atlantic. But there are worse fates; and like the sea-run salmon, the landlocked is a gamefish in every sense—strong and fast, an aerial battler that readily comes to an artificial.

Summers on the lakes of Northern New England, landlocked-salmon fishermen often troll streamer flies or bright spoons or even sewn bait slowly behind their canoes or guideboats. In late spring, when water temperatures are still cool, the salmon often come to the surface to chase baitfish or take hatching insects, and then casting can be rewarding. Every fall, when the spawn begins, landlockeds can be taken in moving water, with the techniques stream trout fishermen use, and this is the climax of the season. But a hot, dry fall may keep the salmon in the lakes until after the legal season shuts down. Fisherman's luck, it's called.

On the Northern Pacific Coast of this continent there are not one but five species of salmon that crowd up into the rivers every summer to lay their eggs. In addition to this variety, and the fact that western salmon don't specifically seek out their birth river, there's another important distinction between these fish and their East-Coast cousins: Pacifics, all of them, die in spectacularly messy fashion after their first and only spawn.

The five Pacific salmon each have at least two popular names, which does nothing to unconfuse fishermen. One set are the names you see on cans of eating salmon, the other is generally the "sporting" names. The biggest and least plentiful of the Pacifics, and one of the most valuable for market and for sport, is the chinook, also known as the **king salmon**.

Found from Northern California up to the Bering Strait, kings are the largest of the salmon and trout family in North America. The current IGFA all-tackle record for kings is a 97-pound four-ounce behemoth that was taken from Alaska's Kenai River in 1985, but there are reliable reports of 120-plus-pounders captured in commercial nets. There are spring, summer and fall runs, but kings are generally the first of the five Pacific salmon to arrive in fresh water, reaching Alaska's Bristol Bay, for example, in June. There, as the spring runoff drops and the streams clear up, these fish become visible—very visible, thanks to their size. Fishermen accustomed to sixteen-inch trout go into mild hysteria the first time they spot a mating pair of these nuclear subs cruising upstream, leaving a wake in four feet of water. To see them approaching while you're wading a small river is to experience the urge to get out of the water and let them pass.

Sheer size and power make them a top gamefish, but of course they're harmless. Still, the worst fright I ever got while fishing was courtesy of a king salmon. A friend and I were fishing a high and muddy Alaskan river, wading deep and casting long, letting our streamer flies swing downstream in the current before retreiving them. Carl was just upriver of me and he was the first to hook up. He yelled "Strike!" I turned to look at him and something unseen in the water cannoned into my knees. Only the level bottom kept me from going in over my head. I staggered back, let out a howl and backpedaled for shore virtually on top of the water. A salmon surfaced in the spot I'd vacated, thrashing frantically against Carl's line. It turned out to be a chinook of only seventeen pounds.

Like all sea-run fish, kings are usually bright upon entering fresh water and over the next month they lose their sheen, turning darker and redder week by week. Males sport tremendous kypes, the hooked lower jaw characteristic of salmonids. Pods of kings work their way upstream for weeks, traveling as much as two thousand miles in the Yukon River. In smaller water they move erratically, resting in the deeper pools, swimming steadily through the channels, gathering below the riffles to take their turn powering through these risky shallows, sometimes with half their bodies showing above the surface. At the headwaters they split up into pairs and sometimes fade back into tiny feeder streams no wider than the fish are long, where they dig their redds and deposit and fertilize their eggs.

Then they die, each and every one.

In the large king rivers such as the Columbia and the Kenai, fishing with heavy tackle from shore or boats is effective, trolling or casting blindly and at long range to cover lots of water. But stalking big kings on foot in small wilderness streams is one of few fishing experiences that give me buck fever. In water so clear you can see the action, you jig your lure or fly past the noses of resting salmon. When one of them moves forward and your line just stops in the water—maybe you've seen the flash of the fish's mouth opening briefly—it's time to set the hook. Hard. Several times. These big ones have a manner reminiscent of a Panama-Canal-class bulldozer, and hooking onto one on light tackle is a straining experience. Twenty or twenty-five pounds is an average size, and they are tough fighters, but the truly big kings, twice that size and more, will stand your hair on end. Even after many weeks in fresh water they keep their strength, and use it well. When you drive the hook home, a big king will often surface (to size up his enemy?), and the sight will weaken your knees. Then you're in for an hour or more of running downstream, hard pulling, frantic reeling and involuntary yells, screams, curses and other expressions of awe as the fish dives, then thrashes on the surface, throwing spray into the treetops with a tail like a snow shovel. If you're very fortunate and make no mistakes, you may land him.

They are not accepted as "real" gamefish, but three of the other four Pacific salmons nevertheless give the angler a decent thrash on rod and reel. **Humpback** salmon—known also as pinks—are relatively small, slab-sided, with almost beak-like jaws and strongly humped shoulders, and excellent table fare when fresh and bright for campers who need a break from Spam. **Chum** salmon, whose other name is dog salmon (because northern native people netted them to feed their dogs in winter), are more plentiful in the lower rivers of western Canada and Alaska. They are bigger than humpies, generally ten to fifteen pounds or so, and alone of the Pacific salmons do not turn crimson to spawn. Instead they develop startling streaks of maroon that extend up their green sides like dull flames licking at a board. In spite of their reputation as "dogs," they will readily take lures and flies and fight for their survival.

The **sockeye**, or red salmon, is the most plentiful in the Northwest. Found from San Francisco northward, it's the one most likely to show up on the label of a can of salmon. It is no trophy even when fresh, but it can be spurred into striking a hook. The sockeye's chief benefit to sportfishermen (and to hunters, netters, conservationists and anyone else interested in preserving the Northwestern ecology) is the sheer size of the annual spawning run. Those millions of fish and the billions of eggs they lay every summer are the prime food source for many other gamefish and for other animals ranging from insects up through birds and foxes to the coastal grizzlies, the brown bears.

Eggs washed by current from the redds tumble downstream like large red BB shot, to the satisfaction of trout, Dolly Varden, grayling and sometimes northern pike that wait below with mouths open. Bears, seals and some birds take the live fish themselves. The salmon that live to spawn contribute too: When their eggs have been deposited, the weeks of hard swimming without food take their toll. By now the salmon are grotesques—thin, mottled red, with wildly humped backs and hooked jaws bristling with sharp teeth. Digestive organs have atrophied to nothing. Fins have worn away to stumps. The flesh seems to peel from their bones. Still struggling against the currents, they eventually turn turtle and hang up in the snags or wash up on the sandbars. Birds and insects pick the carcasses apart, beginning with the eyes. The meat eventually melts away, turning the rivers into protein soup for the microscopic organisms at the base of the food chain. On hot days the rivers may smell like garbage dumps, and the bones of thousands of salmon bleach in the shallows.

Though much smaller than the chinook, the **coho**, the fifth Pacific salmon, gets the vote as Number One Gamefish from many anglers. Its reputation as a hook-and-line battler has led to its successful transplantation into the Great Lakes and waters as far east as Lake Champlain and even a few coastal New England rivers. In its native northwestern rivers it's often known as the silver salmon, a handle that suits it well. In the estuaries or newly arrived in fresh water, these fish are chrome-plated beauties with speed to match. Silvers are extremely valuable fish, for they bring millions of dollars of sportfishing revenue into their regions.

58

A male humpbacked salmon, still sea-bright. David Lambroughton photograph.

An angler carefully unhooks a fly-caught British Columbia steelhead prior to release. David Lambroughton photograph.

Wherever you go to take them, the fishing is often the same: in streams that are low and clear— because silvers normally arrive in the second half of the summer— you look for the fish. They travel in groups of a dozen or so to maybe a hundred, never staying long in one spot and moving fast when under way. They don't swim far from salt water, though. Intercept them from upstream, make your spinner, spoon or streamer dance in front of them at the right depth, and a smash-and-grab strike is almost inevitable. Silvers rarely go bigger than about twelve pounds, which is both a shame and a blessng— they fight with berserk abandon,

and if they reached the size of Atlantic salmon, landing one might become a rare event.

When the silvers are in (a rallying cry, the fisherman's *Surf's Up!*), we sometimes get a little strange. I've watched anglers, particularly ones new to both silvers and the long days of the northern summer, fish until they were exhausted, staggering in the water to hook just one more, to feel the energy of another salmon exploding through the surface and cartwheeling away. Two dozen such hookups in a day will reduce any fisherman to jelly, blubbering but elated. Even as spawning approaches, and the hens turn bronzed and dark and the males go

60

angry red, coho seem to keep their strength, although they do cut down on the aerobatics.

But no sea-run fish gets the kind of respect, if not awe, accorded to the **steelhead**. This is nothing more than a rainbow trout that has taken it into its genes to leave running water, mature at sea or in large lakes, and then return, like a salmon, to lay its eggs. But when you combine the natural style and looks of the river rainbow with the size, strength and feeding habits of a sea predator, you get a gamefish of Atlantic-salmon caliber. (Steelhead fans would put that the other way around, of course.) Like Atlantics, they may return to spawn more than once, but unlike them, they may arrive in their rivers in January as well as in July; there are two distinct strains— summer steelhead and winter steelhead. Both enter fresh water as slim, supercharged steely torpedoes, both darken and develop the rainbow's rose body stripe, until they look like oversize trout.

From northern California up to the Canadian line and in the Great Lakes tributaries, six to fifteen pounds is normal for steelhead, but in the wilds of coastal British Columbia, beware, for— as the old maps used to say— here lie monsters. A few steelhead approaching forty pounds are taken and released every year. Fishermen who go to the trouble and expense to catch such steelhead become emotionally involved with their quarry, and treat them with infinite care. Killing one intentionally is beyond them, and so few of these fish are ever recorded anywhere except on slide film or home video.

Compared to Pacific salmon, steelhead are almost rare, but a network of legal protection is slowly enveloping them. As with the Atlantic salmon, a mystique has grown up about steelhead fishing. These fish do eat— a little— while in their streams, but aggression and curiosity again seem to be the chief motivation behind strikes, even at bait. Summer-run fish often appear in low, clear water, and because they are spooky fish, they must be stalked carefully. On rivers like Oregon's Rogue and Umpqua, fly fishermen often resort to leaders of twelve feet or longer, to put the fly that much farther from the thick line. And long, fine leaders demand much fish-fighting ability from the angler if he ever hopes to land one of these rockets. (Unlike many sea-run fish, steelhead often develop the habit of ducking under snags and other cover when hooked, which doesn't help the fisherman one bit.) Although much steelheading with

FEMALE LAND LOCKED SALMON or QUANANICHE.
(Salmo Salar Sebago. Girard.)

flies calls for wet patterns fished below the surface, often on heavy shooting-taper lines that help cover water quickly, some Canadian rivers carry steelhead that are very willing to come to a large dry fly.

Other rivers, such as the Thompson, in British Columbia, are so big and so wild that fly-fishing is almost out of the question. Big spinning outfits put artificials out to the fish at much less risk to life and limb, but purists are now arming themselves with huge two-handed fly rods, in the European manner, and swimming their flies well even in such tough conditions.

Winter and spring steelheading is very popular, especially in the upper Midwest (although sizable transplants of summer-run fish have taken hold there). As the lake ice breaks up, steelhead cluster around the river mouths, waiting for the slight rise in water temperature that triggers their migration. This seems a particularly masochistic form of sport— wading bone-chilling water, casting in snow and winter wind, numbed fingers trying to chip ice from the line guides— but it's not that different from duck hunting at the same northern latitudes.

61

A common summer sight in coastal Alaskan streams—"reds" moving up-river to spawn, all but oblivious of predators ranging from bears to fishermen. R. Valentine Atkinson photograph.

Following spread:
Fifty-plus pounds of Alaskan king salmon, taken on a medium-weight fly rod. Some Bristol Bay kings turn red even before swimming up into fresh water. Author's photograph.

GAME FISH OF NORTH AMERICA

Shad

HICKORY SHAD (POMOLOBUS MEDIOCRIS)

SO THE SHAD is nothing more than an overgrown herring? Well, on the northeastern coast of the United States, where they know the difference, this silver sea-run fish is often regarded as the poor man's Atlantic salmon. Times have changed, though. Now even comparatively poor (that is, un-rich) fishermen have access to top salmon waters; and even the well-to-do angler knows not to discount the humble shad as a gamefish.

Springtime, when the shadbush blooms white, look for the annual spawning runs to start in coastal rivers around the country. The hickory shad, with its underslung lower jaw, is the southern cousin; although it does reach New England, most of the run is south of the Chesapeake. Like all fish that have spent time at sea, hickories are tough fighters, but they are normally only a couple of pounds. Most popular among sportfishermen is the American shad (white shad), which is commonly five to eight pounds and sometimes goes over ten.

American shad are native to the East Coast, where they range from Maine to Florida. But Seth Green, America's favorite fish planter, brought shad to the West Coast in 1871. He dumped the fry into the Sacramento River, and now they're found from Baja California to Alaska! Northern shad typically spawn more than once, and willingly enter rivers other than their birthplace, so this is a dependably plentiful fishery—at least for the Lower 48, with its dams and pollution.

The top shad rivers are probably the Delaware and the Connecticut, on the East Coast. (The Hudson gets a strong run too, but it is too big to fish easily with rod and reel; small commercial netting outfits take many Hudson shad.) On both coasts the shad runs are virtually social occasions; there are shad festivals, offering lessons in de-boning and filleting the fish, and tasty planked shad and shad roe dishes. But *the* classic shad fishery is the mob scene that takes place below the Enfield Dam, on the Connecticut in Connecticut. Fishermen line up elbow-to-ribs along the concrete spillways, casting lead-head shad darts to the thousands of fish that mill around in frustration, trying to pass upriver. Pandemonium reigns when a fish strikes and cuts across a dozen other lines. Out in the river small boats zoom around, trying to locate the fish channels. Some of the most successful anglers are the brave souls in chest waders who struggle against the swift water and the slippery, unpredictable ledge bottom— if you've got the heart for it, and can anchor yourself slightly upstream and alongside of one of the runs where the fish come through, you can take a shad an hour on a fly or lure. You must find the depth and the slot where the fish want it, and keep your offering there, jigging it occasionally to provoke an aggressive or defensive strike.

But a fish hooked is not a fish landed. Shad have soft mouths and broad, powerful sides that they use effectively in the strong current. Best is to fish with a partner; let him move downstream of you, then drop the fish into his waiting net before the hook pulls out. I am very fond of shad roe and keep a few large hen fish. But one of the largest I lost when the river simply tore the carcass off my belt stringer.

A hickory shad, interrupted on its annual upstream spawning migration. *Joel Arrington* photograph.

Sheefish

ABOUT ALL most of us know about the **sheefish** is that it's usually subtitled "the tarpon of the North." Well, its real name is *inconnu*, or "the unknown." Doesn't help much, does it? Because they are scattered in the rivers and lakes of arctic Canada and in Alaska above the Kuskokwim, few of us ever get a crack at a sheefish, much less catch one. Unknown, indeed.

But prized, and for this same rarity. Anglers who keep a life-list of their catches tend to regard sheefish the way many big-game hunters think of, say, Marco Polo sheep: *Someday I'll get one!*

The facts, however, are these: The sheefish is a genuine salmonid, a whitefish in fact (biologists invariably point out that it is the only *predatory* whitefish), but it does bear a marked resemblance to a tarpon—large, silvery scales, stubbornly outthrust lower jaw, long, slim, powerful body, all wrapped up in a pugnacious package that's quite willing to take a hook and bust up the river. Also like the tarpon, there's something primitive about sheefish, some echo of the prehistoric past. They're salmonids, yes, but they seem to be salmonids whose evolution somehow stopped an age or two ago, leaving them behind their peer group. Like salmon, they spawn in the fall and they swim hundreds of miles upstream to do so, but they don't come in from the sea; they mature in the fresh water of their rivermouths. And like salmon they deposit their eggs on the riverbottoms, but they're broadcast spawners—the female digs no redd, just pumps her spawn into the water. Individual eggs (the ones that aren't eaten) eventually settle between the rocks, where they may or may not be fertilized by a cloud of milt fired off by one of the male fish. Tough-fighting and rough-edged, sheefish always make me think of rowdy dropouts who stayed in the old neighborhood a million years ago while their classmates went on to Darwin U. to become sophisticated salmon.

If you can catch trout, you know how to catch sheefish; you just have to get to the right water and then you have to play the odds, for they are not as numerous as most Alaskan or Canadian gamefish. They are called northern tarpon not only for their looks but also because they jump when hooked, even the big ones of thirty and forty pounds. But as far as I know, such behavior occurs only in streams where the water is skinny; hook a big sheefish in a lake and it'll head for the depths. In any event, you'll be glad you went.

The Alaskan sheefish. These were taken from the Kobuk River, which flows into Kotzebue Sound, western Alaska, just above the Arctic Circle. Ken Alt, Northern Alaska Fisheries Service, photograph.

Trout

THE BRITISH, bless 'em, did more to spread their sort of fishing (and shooting) sports than probably any other group of people on this planet. In Victorian times and earlier, with a disregard for other fish and animal species that would be appalling in today's enlightened society, British military men and commercial travelers and fortune-seekers—those who spent long periods of time away from their homeland—transplanted "their" trout and salmon and gamebirds and red deer and so on all over the planet. While assuring ourselves that *we* would never be so ecologically insensitive—at least now—we may heave a sigh of relief that *they* were, and proceed to enjoy the fruits of their labors.

But bringing fish and animals to North America would be like bringing extra sand to the beach; there was already an eye-popping variety here. Take the noble trout, for example. Of the nine or so true trout on this continent today, only one came from Britain. The trout we most value—the most sought-after as a trophy, conceded, rightly or not, to be the most difficult to catch and thus the best proof of a fisherman's skill—is the **brown trout**, an immigrant from Scotland. The descendants of those fish (brought to America in 1885) are still sometimes classified as Loch Leven browns.

More properly, however, many of our stream-living brown trout, though of European origin, did *not* come from the United Kingdom. While many older anglers still know them as German browns, that designation came into disfavor, for reasons that should be obvious, in the early 1940s. And they were indeed German—the first shipment of their eggs was sent to a hatchery in Long Island, New York, in 1883 by Baron Lucius von Behr.

In April 1984 the centennial anniversary of the first successful planting of these von Behr browns was celebrated by historically accurate reenactment. Members of the Izaak Walton League deposited, from a milk can, two thousand trout fry into the North Branch of Michigan's Pere Marquette River, near the town of Baldwin. On April 11, a

STEELHEAD or SALMON TROUT,
(Salmo Gairdneri, Richardson.)

STEELHEAD or SALMON TROUT,
(Salmo Gairdneri, Richardson.)

century earlier, a certain J.F. Ellis and his assistant, using milk cans, had transferred almost five thousand brown trout fry from a U.S. Fish Commission railcar into the cold, slightly tannic flow of the North Branch. American trout fishing, as has often been said, was changed forever.

The Loch Leven trout, as their name implies, were a stillwater strain, silvery as salmon at certain seasons. The German fish bore the red and black spots and the yellow flanks that today identify a brown trout to us. The two subspecies have interbred, however, as all trout can, and variations among North American browns are generally more due to environmental differences than to genetic traits.

A brown trout in spawning dress is a sight to behold, a gaudy gold and green, red and silver. Larger males develop spectacularly hooked jaws that, in com-

bination with the well-fed brown's broad shoulders and deep body, give them an aggressive appearance. This bullish look is borne out by the way they fight when hooked, often diving deep and slugging it out with massive head-shakings and dodging under snags and around river rocks. Like all trout, both stream- and lake-living browns feed primarily on aquatic insects, which makes them a prime quarry for the fly fisherman. But the larger fish have learned to find protein in bigger chunks—they've become cannibals, ambushing and eating smaller trout, leeches, shiners and other baitfish. (That's how they got so big.) These fish are much more difficult to take on flies, and now the lure and bait fisherman enjoys the upper hand. A large Rapala carefully retreived through a deep, still stream pool represents exactly what such a fish looks for.

A fat, healthy wild brown trout from the Intermountain West. David Lambroughton photograph.

Preceding spread:
A twelve-inch brown trout working steadily in his feeding lane. Dale Spartas photograph.

A heavily spotted Alaskan "leopard" rainbow trout, the caribou-hair mouse fly that took it still stuck in its wood-hard jaw. Author's photograph.

A silvery, lightly marked West-Coast rainbow trout. Contrast this fish with the rainbow on the facing page; variations in color, size and shape may exist from one river's population to the next when barriers keep species from intermingling. David Lambroughton photograph.

An American classic-the native Western rainbow trout. Jim & KittyVincent photograph.

In friendly comparisons, when every judgement of speed and color and fighting ability has been made, brown-trout fans eventually play their trump card—that browns, especially those big ones, are caught far less often than rainbows or brookies. Which makes them more of a challenge, a truly superior gamefish. There's some truth to this, but remember that unlike their two popular cousins browns are generally nighttime feeders, while we are generally daytime anglers. Think back to the really monstrous. browns you've seen, in newspaper photos or brought dripping into tackle shops on opening day: weren't most taken in the black of night, or by snot-nosed kids fishing deep with nightcrawlers? There's a lesson to be learned here.

Rainbow trout, by contrast, are native Yankees, although Westerners who were moved East (not to mention all over the

rest of the planet, from Argentina to New Zealand to Europe) as their sterling qualities became known. Unlike many salmonids, wild rainbows are generally springtime spawners. They also cross-breed readily with other species, and of all the trouts accept the widest range of water temperatures and quality. This makes the rainbow the darling of the biologists and has led to many hybrids and sub-subspecies and hatchery experiments. The nonfishing public who sees trout only on a plate, garnished with lemon, would recognize the rainbow; many frozen supermarket trout are 'bows, often reared, harvested and flash-frozen in the Orient. And stream trout these days are often hatchery rainbows, pale, cookie-cutter fish mass-produced and released annually to satisfy the increasing demands of the fishing public. It's a testament to the rainbow's style that even these fish

76

THE CANADIAN RED TROUT
FEMALE

strike a fly or lure (or baited hook) with a certain dash.

But a wild rainbow is a gamefish to be reckoned with—a hunter that pounces like a cat and then gyrates wildly away across the top of the water when insulted with a hook. In fact, in western Alaska there's a strain of rainbows so heavily spotted and so predatory they are called leopard trout. The name fits. Some of the finest fishing I've had was there, twitching a caribou-hair mouse across the shallow coastal streams, swinging the fly out from the bank like a real mouse trying desperately to reach the far shore. A hungry rainbow would accelerate away, betraying its lie under the bank with a sudden swirl, and arc out into the current after the mouse, engulfing it from behind with its wide, white open mouth showing clearly against the green water. But some trout seemed to want to play, charging the struggling "mouse" five or six times before leaping upon it, sometimes even slapping it clear out of the water with their tails.

The trout's namesake rainbow is the slash of color that decorates its flanks. This may be a wide band of stunning hot pink or just a pale rosy track or simply an irregular boundary between zones of spots on the fish's back and sides. The rest of the fish may be deep green above, fading through yellow to a white belly, patterned with irregular black specks, or—particularly near salt water—blazing silver with hardly any specks at all. Rainbows can show remarkable variation from one river or lake to another, never mind from region to region and season to season, and there are dozens of different strains. Some migrate readily to open water such as lakes or even the sea, others remain resident in their rivers year-round. And the potential for tremendous growth is there too: Canadian fisheries biologists report netting a rainbow of more than 52 pounds in a lake in British Columbia.

THE CANADIAN RED TROUT
ADULT MALE

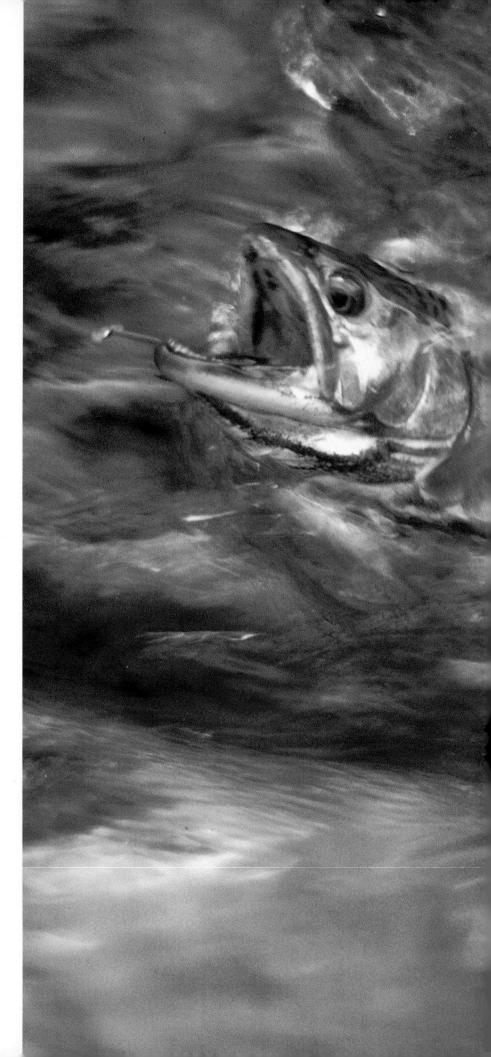

The connoisseur's choice, however, may be the seemingly shy and retiring **brook trout**. Another American, the brookie evolved in the northeastern corner of the continent, and is considered the native trout from Labrador down through New England and into the southern Appalachians. Because the brookie was the only trout in New England before the 1880s, and New England, as the oldest white-settled region of America, was the birthplace of American fly-fishing, the brook trout figures heroically in our sportfishing history. Records from the 19th Century indicate that "squaretails" of eight and nine pounds were taken every year in the States; but today, even in the remote streams and lakes of northern Maine, a three-pounder makes the local newspapers.

It's a judgement call, but I think the brook trout is the most beautiful of America's gamefish. Delicate and jewel-like in small sizes, awesome and powerful as large fish, brookies are spectacularly colored—aquatic versions of the male wood duck. Their lower fins are red-gold, edged in black and white, and in male fish, particularly at spawning time, this color extends up onto their bellies. Their green-black backs are handsomely decorated with wavy lighter markings, and scattered along their lateral lines are handfuls of red or purple dots within blue halos.

Brook trout are not, of course, "shy and retiring"; merely finicky, demanding cleaner and colder water than other trout. As land is developed, clean, cold waters often become dirty and warmer, and resident brook trout move upstream to the headwaters and then, sometimes, die out. Even under environmental protection, fish grow more slowly in colder water and so it is relatively easy to clean out even a healthy brook trout fishery if angling pressure is high and fish are not released.

Another true native American, the brook trout. Don Blegen photograph.

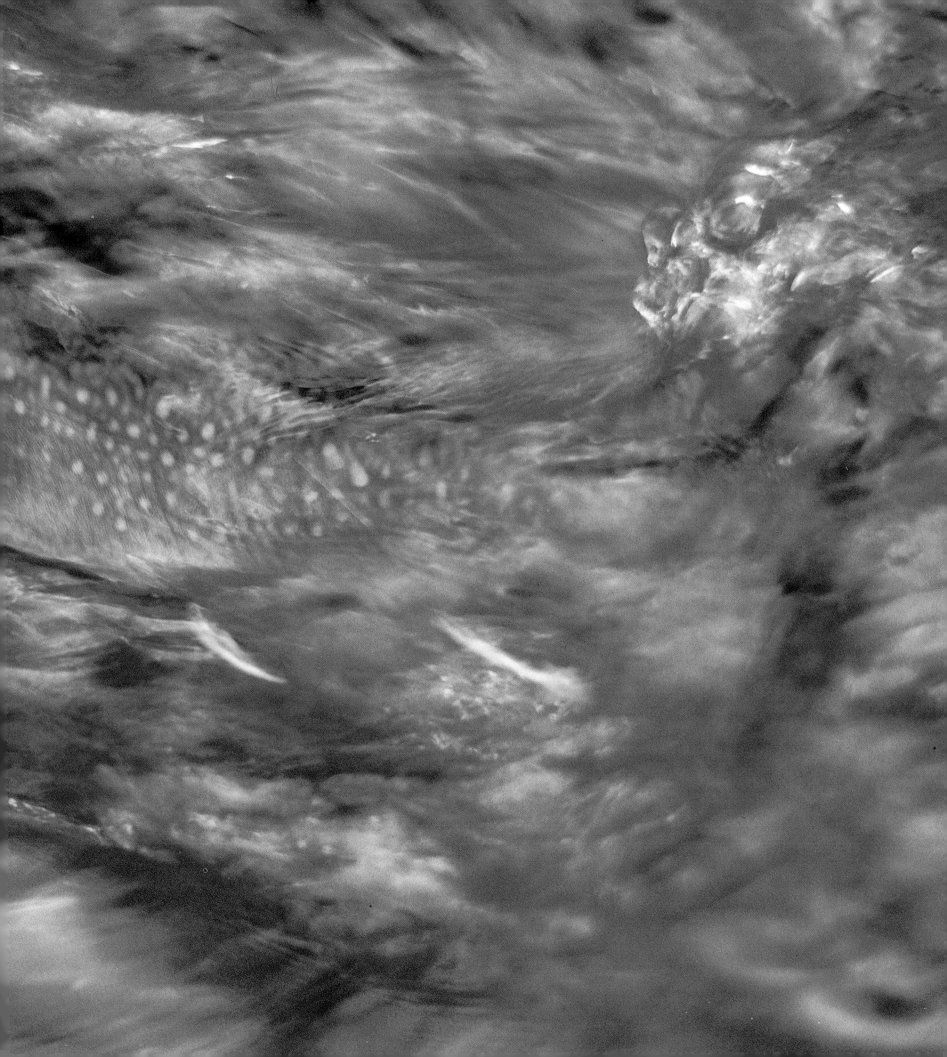

Diver Bill Roston photographed this perfectly marked brook trout charging a fly in a Virginia mountain pond.

In beaver ponds, especially newer ones that haven't silted in yet, you may find hundreds of hungry brook trout willing to compete fiercely for your hook no matter what's on it. This leads to the feeling that the brookie is too dumb for its own good, too ready to sample a lure or bait. However, having been snubbed by many big brook trout, even in unfished wilderness waters, I don't subscribe to this slander at all. Generations of kids have passed their summers dangling worms for eight-inch brookies in the rockbound pools of tiny mountain streams, but truly big brook trout are found in truly big waters. Today's world-record (nine pounds plus) brook trout come from Labrador's Minipi River and Quebec's Broadback watershed, where the "pools" are often lakes connected by short stretches of flowing stream. On calm summer evenings you'll find half a dozen or more brook trout feeding leisurely on huge mayflies. As their backs and dorsal fins arch above the surface, you realize that every one of them is almost as long as your arm. The slightly condescending "brookie" suddenly seems inappropriate.

In the Rocky Mountains the term "native trout" applies to the **cutthroat**, a species that appears in a variety of different forms and colors, each named for its region. Many anglers know the Yellowstone cutthroat and the Snake River cutts, but there are also strong cutthroat populations on the West Coast, from California up through British Columbia into Alaska, some of which spend part of their lives at sea, returning like salmon to lay their eggs in rivers, and some of which stay in fresh water. (Other recognized and officially classified strains of cutthroat include the Westslope, Humboldt, Paiute, Greenback, Bonneville, Rio Grande, Colorado River, Lahontan and Willow Creek.) Like most rainbows, cutthroat trout spawn in the spring; biologically they may in fact be closer to rainbows than to other trout, as the two species interbreed readily.

The lurid name comes not from any Jack-the-Ripper feeding (or mating!) tendencies but from the red-orange markings, often a vivid slash, behind and below the cutthroat's lower jaw. On some fish, particularly Yellowstone cutts, the marking is much more than a simple slash, extending upward into a red blush that covers almost the entire opercle, or "cheek."

Even cutthroat partisans concede that their fish is not a premier fighter or spectacular jumper on rod and reel, but it is nevertheless a worthy gamefish that can be taken on a variety of tackle. Like the brook trout, cutthroat sometimes suffer from a reputation for airheadedness, a suicidal willingness to take lure or bait. I invite people who believe that to fish any stillwater section of, say, the Yellowstone River, where big (*big*) cutthroat will rise majestically from their lies, inspect your offering with the deliberation of arms negotiators, then smugly sink back to the bottom, where they will go on feeding leisurely on nymphs and other naturals. In fast water cutthroats can be a piece of cake, but in those conditions, when a fish has only a split second to inspect any passing item that might be food, many other trout mistakenly grab artificials also. A favorite technique is to cast a grasshopper imitation right to the streambank and then float/twitch it away, like a hopper that was blown into the drink and is trying to make it to shore.

Perhaps the best thing about cutts is the waters in which they are found—from mossy rain-forest streams of the Pacific Northwest to the mountain lakes and rivers of the Continental Divide. Their tendency to evolve into distinct strains when isolated by natural barriers makes them something of a "collector's trout," prized by fishermen who scorn the trout mass-produced by hatcheries.

But the cutt is a people's trout, too. Perhaps you, like me, are one of the millions of tourists who have hung over the railings of Fishing Bridge in Yellowstone National Park, admiring the sinuous trout swimming gracefully below. Those too are cutthroats.

If the brook trout has a serious rival for the title of Most Gorgeous, it is the **golden trout**, which originated in the Kern River system of California's Sierra Nevada range. Although the fish has been propagated by hatcheries and subsequently distributed throughout several Western states, it survives only in cold, high-altitude mountain lakes and streams. Reaching golden-trout waters usually means backpacking or horsepacking into a remote area and spending at least one night on the hard ground; for most of us, this only increases the allure of this striking and somewhat rare trout.

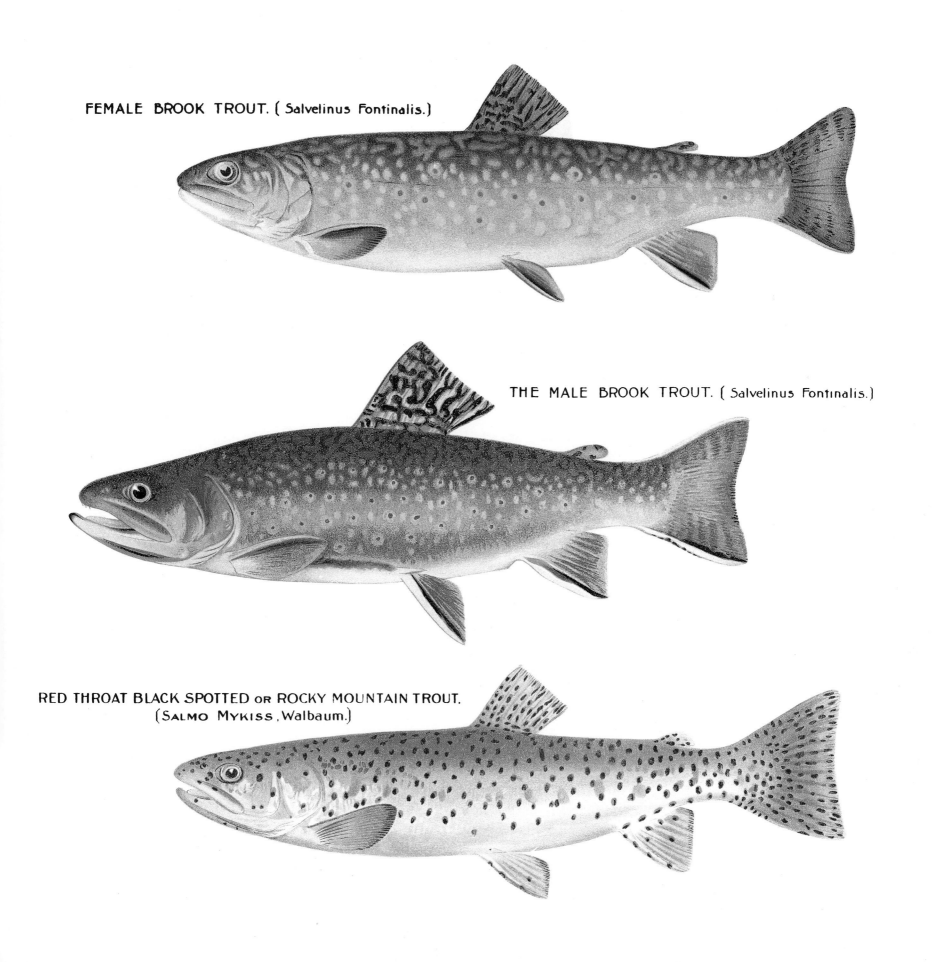

FEMALE BROOK TROUT. (Salvelinus Fontinalis.)

THE MALE BROOK TROUT. (Salvelinus Fontinalis.)

RED THROAT BLACK SPOTTED OR ROCKY MOUNTAIN TROUT.
(SALMO MYKISS, Walbaum.)

What the great lakes of the subarctic Canadian shield are famous for—giant lake trout. Northwest Territories photograph.

To describe the golden in words leaves the impression that this fish is a freak, a garish leftover from some genetic experiment. How else to explain a trout that looks like a conflagration of crimson, yellow, green, black and creamy white, all in shades that can only be described as *intense*? All combined with a heavily black-spotted tail and dorsal fin and a row of leftover parr markings, those vertical stripes that disappear from other trout as they mature. All I can tell you is that it works—the golden trout shimmers in the high-altitude sun in complete harmony with itself and its mountain environment. It's interesting to note that biologists who have raised goldens at lower altitudes find that the fish grows up a much more normal silvery-blue color.

The charrs are a genus of arctic salmonids that often cause considerable confusion among fishermen trying to keep scientific names, popular names and even appearances straight. But for our purposes they are simply trout—efficient predators, superb tackle-busters and thus great gamefish. And you don't need to travel to the far north to take charr, either; the eastern brook trout happens to be a charr, and so is the deep-dwelling lake trout.

Of all our salmonids, the **lake trout** is regularly surpassed in size only by the Pacific chinook (king) salmon. In the Great Lakes, where these trout were an important commercial fish before the lamprey plague drastically reduced the population, netters occasionally report lake trout of a hundred pounds or more, but a rod-and-reel fish of half that size is remarkable. Lake trout are widely distributed across almost all of Canada (where they're sometimes called gray trout), even well up into the Arctic islands, and from the Maritime coast west into Alaska to Bristol Bay (the local name is mackinaw). In the Lower 48, lake trout occur naturally only from northern New England (in Maine they're called togue) and upstate New York to the Great Lakes region. Lake trout have been transplanted, however, as far west and south as northern California.

Even more so than brookies, lakers demand cold water and they generally inhabit deep, clear, well-oxygenated lakes with good smelt populations. They are the premier gamefish of the tremendous lakes of the central Canadian shield—Great Bear, Great Slave, Athabaska and others—and anglers come from around the world to troll and cast for these huge wilderness lakers. In warmer climates, lake trout escape midsummer temperatures by living at depths of a hundred feet or more (sometimes much more), and about the only way to show them a lure is with deep-sinking leadcore line or even diving outriggers. Fish caught this way don't always put up much of a battle, but in colder waters or seasons—during the fall spawn, for example—when lake trout are often found in the shallows around rivermouths, they can be taken on lighter tackle. The main attraction of the laker, however, is always its size; they are usually two, three, maybe five times bigger than any other trout in their lakes, and older too.

Dolly Varden are western charr, found in great numbers especially in the streams of Alaska and the Northwest that Pacific salmon return to for spawning. Like the coastal rainbows, these Dollies feed voraciously on salmon eggs, and commercial fishermen claim they make a sizable dent in the salmon fingerling populations as well. This behavior—plus a certain natural boldness—has helped hatch the idea that Dolly Varden are freshwater sharks. Unfortunately, even dedicated catch-and-release sportsmen often regard Dollies as second-class citizens, treating them as "lunch fish." (As it happens, clean-water Dolly Varden taste wonderful, with a delicate flavor to their rosy pink meat. But perhaps anything cooked over an open fire on a streambank tastes better.)

But nevertheless they can be game fighters, and Dollies of ten pounds or more are common, at least in less-fished drainages. Dolly Varden like fast-flowing cold water. They're often caught in the shallow riffles below deeper pools, where the oxygen content is high and where anything (such as those salmon eggs) washing down from upstream is readily visible. They are often as gaudy as any trout, with white-edged fins, blazing orange-yellow bellies and white- or even lavender-spotted sides and bronze-green backs. The story goes that these fish are named after Dolly Varden, a character in Charles Dickens's *Barnaby Rudge* who supposedly also wore lavender spots. However, a friend who researched the matter claims that Dolly's dress is described only as cherry-colored; he thinks it more likely that—for example—a gold-rush miner

Happiness is almost twelve pounds of Alaskan Dolly Varden. Author's photograph.

Photographer Tim Leary captured the telltale "bloody" gill covers and lower jaw of the cutthroat trout.

Following spread:
A looking-glass view of a hooked Oregon cutthroat trout. Don Blegen photograph.

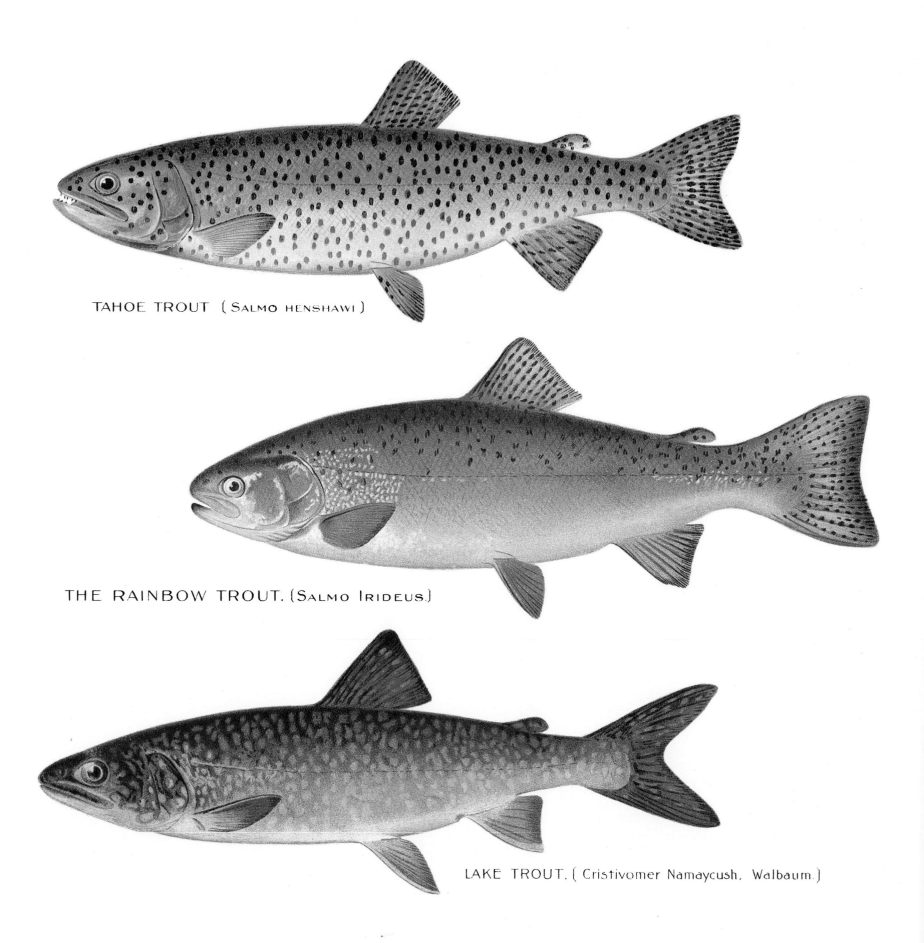

TAHOE TROUT (Salmo henshawi)

THE RAINBOW TROUT. (Salmo Irideus.)

LAKE TROUT. (Cristivomer Namaycush, Walbaum.)

THE BROWN TROUT. (Salmo Fario.)

who read Dickens evenings in his shack romantically named his claim "The Dolly Varden" (Dolly being a popular Victorian name). Then perhaps these fish were discovered in the stream nearby and picked up their name by association. . . . Well, it's a long shot. But no one's come up with a better explanation.

The **Arctic charr** is another coldwater northern salmonid, often similar enough in appearance to the Dolly Varden to cause confusion. In eastern Canada the fish is often found in brook trout water, and newcomers who see only the spectacularly colored bellies and fins of both fish find them hard to tell apart also. Arctic charr lack the worm-like black-on-green markings that brookies carry on their backs; and while charr may have no spots at all, the spots on any charr (brook trout included, remember) are light-colored while the spots of true trout are dark.

Distinguishing Arctics from Dollies is another matter. The rule of thumb is that if the spots on the fish are smaller than the iris of its eyes, then it's a Dolly Varden. However, as their ranges overlap only from central Canada westward, it's generally safe to say that an eastern charr—taken in Labrador, let's say, or Quebec, is indeed a charr and not a Dolly.

The charr is also a bold predator, often seemingly unafraid of man. Twice I've lost small grayling to charr that dashed out from the shadows to rip the fish off my hook. And a charr once bit me while I was squatting in the shallows, cleaning a grayling for the table. A gill raker was caught on my finger: I held my hand out into the current and tried to shake it away, and a six-pound charr rushed up and obligingly ripped it off. How do I know he was six pounds? While the fish hung in the current a yard out, chewing the morsel down and eyeing me hungrily, another fisherman extended his rod tip out over my head and dapped a streamer in front of the charr's nose. He took it unhesitatingly and shortly thereafter joined the grayling in the frying pan.

"A good gamefish is too valuable to be caught only once." This wild rainbow is receiving proper and careful handling as it is released; even the dog seems respectful. Author's photograph.

SALTWATER

FISH

Saltwater Fish

OCEAN FISH are, pound for pound, about a whole order of magnitude tougher than their inland counterparts. And the only way I can think of to explain this sounds suspiciously Disneyesque: Life is that much harder in the sea that its inhabitants just naturally grow up leaner and meaner. But this is pure Darwinism, too—when the going gets tough, the tough get going. And so it is. The amazing diversity of life in the ocean means that virtually every saltwater fish has something to fear—is the target of some predator, if not of a host of different predators—and is in turn feared by something else. Sharks, seals, toothed eels, barracuda, striped bass, bluefish, all the tunas, swordfish, marlin, porpoises, dolphin, bonito, mackerel, drum—the list is exceedingly long, but all these creatures chase each other and many smaller species around. Then add in a fleet of sharp-billed predatory seabirds that are also perenially hungry, and you begin to get the picture. Speed means the difference between eating and being eaten. Speed equals survival.

Note too that there are no stocked fish, no hatchery potatoes, at sea; these are wild fish, with all their behavior patterns and genetic structures intact.

It's true too that many saltwater fish have no "homes." A trout or inland bass usually establishes a base from which to sally forth on short feeding excursions; if they move from their protective lies behind rocks or blowdowns at all, it is often only for a few feet or so. The exception might be their travels during spawning season, but even these journeys pale in comparison to the roving that sea-species such as stripers, tuna, sharks and many others are accustomed to. This continual movement may itself make such fish both hungrier and stronger. It may also affect the way a fish responds to hook and line—not bound by the confines of a stream (as well as perhaps by the inner confines of this nesting instinct), an ocean fish has more room to run and fight.

A major factor that contributes greatly to the "gameness" of saltwater gamefish is simply their size. In many North American lakes and streams, a ten-pound fish is remarkable enough to make the local newspaper. But of course ten pounds or so is about where many ocean fish start; and ten pounds of something hardly makes decent bait for some big-game species.

No one disputes that a six-hundred-pound bluefin, or a one-hundred-pound tarpon, or even a thirty-pound channel bass is a cranky customer to subdue and bring to hand. But my own introduction to the toughness of saltwater fish came at the hands (fins?) of something much, much smaller.

I was driving along the Connecticut shore of Long Island Sound and spotted activity in the water just off a cluster of rocks. I was employed by a tackle company at the time and therefore had with me a prototype saltwater fly rod. Rated for a ten-weight fly line, it was made of the new miracle material called graphite; to me, accustomed to fishing willowy split-cane rods with #5 lines on them, it seemed an elephant gun. But I eagerly rigged up and raced down onto the rocks and began to cast a large streamer fly. Bang! *A strike right away! Love this saltwater fishing!* The big rod bent heavily in my hands as something tried to escape. I was shocked to discover that my fish was all of a foot long; and I was so green I had to ask, somewhat reluctantly, another fisherman what it was. What it was was a bluefish, they of the teeth and appetite, but one so small it was referred to locally as a snapper. (Full-sized blues are known there, more respectfully, as choppers.) But it made a strong and lasting impression on me, for that twelve-inch fish had exercised my nine-and-a-half-foot saltwater rod as much or maybe more than a twelve-inch brown trout would have my seven-and-a-half-foot bamboo rod, back home in the mountains of Vermont.

There's another aspect of sea-fishing that tends to jar the senses of the transplanted freshwater angler: the vastness of the ocean. Even an inshore tidal flat may be huge, acreage far larger than any stream or pond or lake. You may wonder, in fact, just what on earth you're doing when you stand for the first time in the bow of a boat, rod in hand, staring out at what seems a great desert of heaving water. (If you really want to feel foolish, do it with a fly rod; how can you cope with that everpresent wind, those huge distances?) Offshore there might be hundreds of feet of water *below* you—a dimension you may hardly have considered before.

In a stream—shallow, neatly confined, reachable—there's current to read, rocks and logs and banks to cast to, fish feeding visibly nearby. But streams are at a premium now; they're becoming more crowded daily. The fishing fleet on our lakes and ponds is growing too. But new—really new—fishing grounds are still regularly being discovered in salt water.

It takes time and experience to learn the ocean, or that infinitesimally small part of it that you fish, but eventually your eyes open to the clues. Sometimes it's easy—a cloud of gulls wheeling and diving into water boiling with herring desperate to escape a school of tuna attacking from beneath. Or a floating log or piece of ship's debris that draws fish to it like a magnet. Other times it might be nothing more than "nervous water," that slight disturbance of the surface that betrays fish to the experienced eye. Inshore, tide becomes a major factor. On our northern coasts, the variation may be fifteen vertical feet. Interested in surfcasting? Walk your beach at high tide, then at dead low, then at every stage inbetween. Unless you know where the rocks are, and the barrier reefs and the drop-offs, how can you know where the currents will rip, where the bait will be carried, and ultimately where the gamefish will congregate? Certainly you can simply appear one day or night, rod in hand, and walk over to where "the other guys" are casting. You might even strike up a conversation that leads to a friendship that provides you with some of what the experienced fisherman has learned. Nothing wrong with that—just make sure that one day you give him something of equal value in return.

But to address the sport itself, the fishing and the trophy: When it all comes together for you—when your first tarpon rockets into the air with its gills rattling and gyrates away like a rodeo bronc, when a great bull of a striped bass opts to take your plug to the Sea of Japan, when a hundred pounds of sailfish thrashes its shimmering dorsal fin in defiance of your hook—you will find yourself approaching that plane of existence known only to the true elitist. The man or woman who sets high standards, who lives by a code, for whom that fragile fishing line is a direct connection to life, death—and great beauty.

GAME FISH OF NORTH AMERICA

Barracuda

A Florida Keys barracuda; note the protective glove. R. Valentine Atkinson photograph.

THE PIKE OR MUSKIE of the tropics is of course the **barracuda**, a much-maligned gamefish that deserves better treatment than it gets. Thanks to its reputation as a rapacious killer, every schoolchild can recognize a barracuda, and hordes of inexperienced snorkelers have made dramatic exits from the water upon sight of even a small 'cuda. But attacks upon humans, even those wearing the fabled "flashing jewelry," are extremely rare.

(By comparison, sharks are wanton maneaters, yet even shark attacks are far more rare than, say, being struck by lightning on the golf course.)

Even a small barracuda has prominent teeth, and big barracuda are notably curious. The combination results in a deadly looking marine predator that may follow a diver—or your lure—like a Labrador retreiver. Don't worry unduly; I've never heard of a wading fisherman who was struck by a barracuda (or a shark, for that matter). Instead, put that curiosity to good use in fishing. Barracuda get their best shot at us while we're removing our hooks from their lips; wear gloves and use pliers.

The bigger a barracuda is, the less likely you are to hook him. Fish up to about twenty pounds are relatively easy

to take. Fifty-pounders are sometimes caught by trolling along deeper reefs or wrecks offshore. Barracuda of one hundred pounds—perhaps seven feet long—are known to exist, but are almost impossible to bring to a hook. The IGFA, for example, lists the official all-tackle world record as only eighty-three pounds. Fortunately for us, even smaller barracuda are berserk fighters on rod & reel, sometimes displaying a desperate strength and abandon that leaves me wondering how such horsepower can be packed into this slim, almost insubstantial animal. To escape a hook, or sometimes in pursuit of food, barracuda will make incredible leaps, more like long, shallow racing dives than the insane vertical pirouettes of a tarpon. A fisherman I know swears he hooked a barracuda that promptly broke him off by jumping clear over a mangrove bush.

The sight-fisherman, whether he chooses spoons, plugs or streamer flies, can easily find barracuda while stalking the inshore lagoons and flats that also teem with bonefish, snook, redfish and so on. Barracuda don't roam constantly, the way other flats fish do, so a greenish, slim shape holding position over the bottom is usually a 'cuda. Present your fly or lure near enough to catch its attention, but not too close or the fish will simply vanish. Experience is the best teacher. You'll never really see a barracuda strike—one moment the fish is motionless, studying your offering, and then magically the lure is gone. And unless you've rigged up with a wire shock tippet, it may well be gone for good.

A barracuda taken on the coral flats; note the wire tippet, insurance against slashing teeth. Joel Arrington photograph.

Billfish

GAME FISH OF NORTH AMERICA

THE TERM "BILLFISH" covers several species of superb game animals that often reach stupendous size, live in deep water that affords them cubic acres of fighting room, have the combative disposition to put that room to use while attached to a fishing line, and that have pointy noses. There's something about billfish that makes people want to hang them on a wall, too; it may simply be that they look absolutely grand—deep-chested, long, tapering bodies decorated with fins that are either large and graceful or wickedly scimitar-like. A very distant relative (by marriage) once held the black marlin world record; he had the entire fish mounted and displayed on the wall of a restaurant in Palm Beach—all 1,400-plus pounds of it.

Billfish are not always so heavy, but their reputation precedes them. Much more recently, another acquaintance set out to become a billfisherman. His construction business had prospered, so he was able to take delivery of a 38-foot Bertram, which he then outfitted in grand style with all manner of expensive tackle and accessories. His first sortie, off Montauk, began well. All the outriggers and rods were working, with baits and lures and teasers out everywhere astern. For hours they trolled the waves, my friend slowly working himself into a lather of anticipation. At last, something caught his attention and he left the bridge to look. Right there, almost under the transom, a white marlin was chasing one of the teasers! While he watched, the long shape rose in the water and slashed at the hookless decoy with its bill. This was it! But none of the trolling rods had lures anywhere nearby!

He looked wildly around. In the "rocket launcher" was a spare outfit, a heavy rig, with 80-pound line and a huge reel. He grabbed it, rushed to the stern, flopped the ready lure into the water. And here, almost under his nose, the first marlin of his career rose to the offering and unhesitatingly attacked it.

Breathing hard, Al made ready. He locked the drag. He spread his feet, braced his back, counted slowly out loud, flexed his big hands on the rod.

Blue marlin. Lefty Kreh photograph.

A hooked blue marlin tries again to sound as it is brought to the boat. Douglas Perrine photograph.

Struck, hard! And yanked the astonished marlin clean out of the water and over his shoulder, where it thudded into the cockpit of the Bertram. It was all of about sixty pounds.

Al was so disappointed and so enraged he just planted his feet, bunched up his huge shoulders, and cast the fish back over the transom into the sea. He flipped the reel into free-spool and bellowed at the doubly bewildered marlin, "Now get out there and FIGHT!"

The moral of the story is that not all billfish are the size of compact cars. Most, in fact, are not. The International Game Fish Association's Thousand Pound Club, which was formed in January, 1985, had fewer than 150 members three years later, and many of those qualified with bluefin tuna or sharks. Most, however, were marlin, and almost all were **black marlin**, the sportfishing kings of the family. (Although commercial longliner fishermen say that their catches indicate blue marlin grow larger.) Like most marlins, blacks are migratory deep-sea fish. They prefer tropical waters and are normally found only in the Pacific and Indian oceans. Current world-record blacks are caught in Australian waters, but Hawaii and Baja Mexico offer black marlin fishing as well. Giant blacks especially are blocky, awesome creatures, but all are dark blue above and silvery below, with the only pectoral fins in the marlin family that cannot fold flat against the body. They are seemingly inexhaustible fighters on rod and reel, and big-game fishing is full of true tales of epic battles lasting hours and hours, proceeding from elation through determination to tears, fatigue and, sometimes, a resolve never to do this again.

Striped marlin are also Pacific and Indian Ocean fish that move seasonally in search of warmer water. Striped marlin have high, prominent dorsal fins and are sleeker and more streamlined than their black cousins, which may relate to the fact that they are generally spectacular aerial fighters. Some fishermen swear striped marlin spend more time out of the water than in when hooked, and they are known for their "greyhounding," runs of ten or more long, shallow linked jumps that may take the fish through ninety degrees of the compass and the fisherman to the edge of credulity. All marlin have vertical bars on their backs and sides, but they are more prominent on this fish.

Few striped marlin reach five hundred pounds. The other giant subspecies is the **blue marlin**, which inhabits both the Pacific and Atlantic oceans. Thousand-pounders, always females, have been taken in Hawaii, the Virgin Islands and as far north as Cape Hatteras, but Pacific blues are generally larger. Some biologists regard the Pacific and Atlantic versions as different species., but both are silvery white below the midline, a deep, rich blue above, and often bear faint light-blue vertical stripes. There is a difference in the density of the lateral-line markings of the two, however.

The Atlantic marlin is the **white marlin**, a relative baby as billfish go. A 200-pounder would go straight into the sportfishing record books (as long as it was caught on "legal" tackle, of course). Although whites are routinely caught as far north as Cape Cod, as always the larger specimens occur in warmer water, in the Bahamas and clear down to Venezuela and Brazil. White marlin have rounded fin-tips and high dorsals, are normally light in color and often tend toward green instead of blue, and have sharply delineated lateral lines.

Sailfish are also relatively small, but they are spectacular-looking, thanks to their shimmering huge dorsal fans and streamlined bodies, and very popular light-tackle gamefish. This is the fish that was seemingly made for waiting room walls, so popular with the more casual fishermen that taxidermists keep hundreds of fiberglass blanks on hand, ready to ship out at a phone call's notice. In the record books, Pacific sailfish approach 200 pounds and Atlantic sails, in a different category, top out at about 130 pounds, but taxonomists are beginning to believe that they are one species. And recently, Japanese catch records studied by the National Marine Fisheries Service were found to indicate that Atlantic sailfish also grow to 175 pounds or so—they just haven't been taken on rod and line yet.

By definition a billfish, although a different family than the marlins, the broadbill **swordfish** is also an Atlantic species. (In fact, it is found worldwide.) Females grow to a thousand pounds or more, but most swordfish are half that or less. They are instantly distinguishable from marlin by their high, stiff dorsal fin and, naturally, their sword, which is about one-third longer and wider than that of a comparable marlin. Although they have a reputation

Atlantic sailfish. Joel Arrington photograph.

as easily spooked and wary, swordfish are also notably aggressive predators who strike and slash their way merrily through schools of large baitfish. There are dozens of verified cases of swordfish attacking boats, the best known being the big one that attacked the research submarine *Alvin* at almost 2,000 feet down. Perhaps because it resembles a giant eye, the fish struck at a viewing port on the sub's flank; the sword glanced off and buried itself almost completely in the cladding of the hull, where it stuck. *Alvin* rose to the surface, dragging the fish with it, and the crew enjoyed swordfish steaks for some days.

With the exception of swordfish, American sportfishermen do not often eat big bills, except maybe as a ritual post-kill meal. In a way it's a shame, for all these fish but the striped mariin, which has red meat, have firm, light-colored flesh that brings high prices in other parts of the world. More and more billfish are being released alive, thanks to the conservation efforts of such groups as The Billfish Foundation, but there is some question as to just how many fish, exhausted by hours-long battles, revive soon enough to swim and breathe normally and to survive shark attacks.

Serious marlin fishing is to plain-old fishin' as Formula One Grand Prix racing is to Sunday driving. To get involved, you can play the multimillion-dollar "goldplater" game, with its custom-built boats and sophisticated tackle and full-time professional crews who shuttle your craft around the world's oceans from tournament to tournament (where you then arrive in your jet). Or you may simply take yourself to a billfish hotspot— Kona, Hawaii, or Bimini, in the Bahamas, or Cabo San Lucas, Baja, maybe—and hire a charter captain for a day or a week. He will know where in the blue water to go, what sort of combination of gaudy lures, sewn baits, cabled hooks and teasers to troll at what depth and speed, and how to wear out the fish with his boat throttles when you get a hook-up. As a once-in-a-lifetime experience, it can't be beat.

A black marlin is captured in the Gulf-stream off Florida. The fish will not be released; it will be dragged aboard through the port in the boat's transom. Roy Attaway photograph.

If you're interested in doing it yourself, there are inbetweens. A boat is a prime necessity, although sailfish are occasionally caught from piers. Heavy tackle for heavy fish, too, although even fly fishermen now pursue billfish. Learning where marlin are found is no different than learning where the trout fishing is good in a stream—make the right friends and exchange help and information. Learn what to look for: Swordfish sometimes bask on the surface (that's why they can be harpooned commercially); groups of sailfish surround baitfish schools and bunch them up on top for slaughter. The giant marlin eat squid, wahoo, tuna, dolphin, mullet, you name it. Learn which inexpensive reels can take the punishment, which lines, which knots, which hooks, and ease into this sport of kings economically. It can be done, and the reward is someday finding yourself connected by a slender thread to one of earth's great creatures.

There are great and tantalizing uncertainties, too. Picture yourself trolling slowly through the black night, your boat rocking across long swells that were born in the great ocean basin a thousand miles away. Beneath your keel is the precipitous edge of a submarine canyon; here the fathometer reads 300 feet but ten feet farther over it plunges to 3,000 feet. And far below and behind swims your carefully prepared bait, a mackerel with a bioluminescent lightstick—and a pair of deadly sharp fist-sized hooks—sewn into its belly. Like the tethered goat bleating to a tiger, the mackerel swings from side to side through the inky depths, its eerie greenish light not visible topsides, where all is peaceful.

When the strike comes, when you have eased into the fighting chair and snugged the thick rod into your harness, the reel ticking faster and faster as line peels out all the while, when you arch back and finally feel the surprise and anger and power at the far end—in the gloom you wonder. Is it the swordfish you hope for, or is it . . . what?

A sailfish leaps to throw the hook. Roy Attaway photograph.

Bluefish

WHEN THEY'RE LITTLE they are called snappers; when they grow up big and strong, they're known as choppers. That pretty much summarizes the **bluefish**'s approach to life. If blues grew as big even as little sharks, no one would go in the water when the annual run comes up the coasts, following the summer warming trend north like Attila's Huns pushing into Europe. (As it is, every year a few swimmers lose toes or wind up in coastal emergency rooms with bluefish slashes.) People who should know report that schools measuring twenty square miles have been seen in the Atlantic—presumably hewing a miles-wide path of destruction that might leave the average plague of locusts gasping in admiration. When the bluefish are on top, it's no trick to find them: From a distance, the first clue is a school of seabirds wheeling and diving at the surface; as the fisherman approaches, he may see myriad flashes of silver on the water—thousands of

panicked baitfish jumping for their lives as the blues slash at them from below. And the water boils and quivers with the life (and death) within.

Catching a bluefish, or even a cooler-full, at such times is no challenge. The feeding fish will strike literally anything, even bare hooks, if they are big and shiny enough to attract attention. As you might expect, bluefish of any size—they occasionally reach twenty-five to thirty pounds—fight like demons when hooked. All this makes the blue a particularly attractive fish for newcomers to salt water, for saltwater fly fishermen who otherwise could search for days for a fish to cast to, and for those looking to load up the freezer. Sometimes the problem is catching too many fish; when the madness is on, the dedicated fisherman might find it difficult to stop obliging these voracious feeders.

When the schools dive, sometimes for weeks, finding them is a matter of luck.

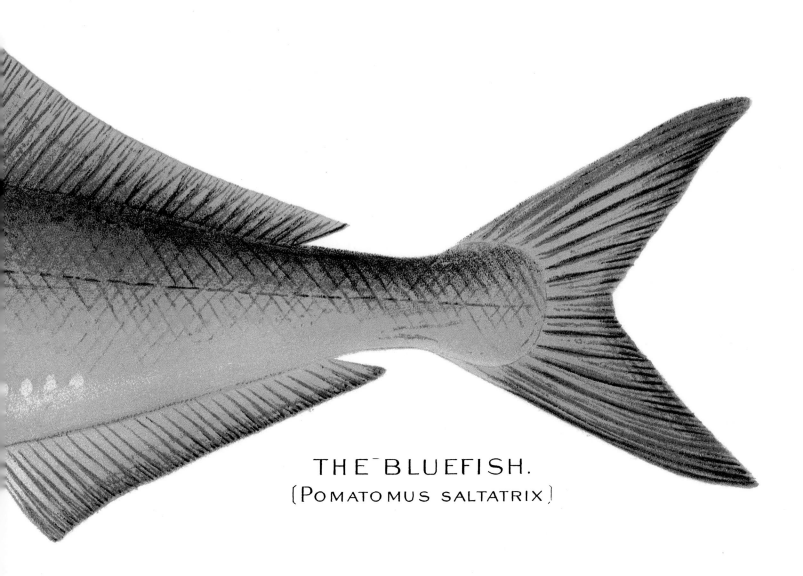

THE BLUEFISH.
(POMATOMUS SALTATRIX)

The word spreads quickly, though, once someone makes contact, and soon everyone is at it again, now with heavily weighted and baited tackle.

Blues are handsome fish, silvery to blue-black, streamlined, fast swimmers, with oversize jaws that boast rows of large, needle-sharp teeth. Unhooking them safely requires gloves, a stout grip, and long-jawed pliers. Some people prefer to deliver the last rites with a "priest" before handling bluefish, but anyone who fishes for them more than casually soon bears a few scars. Beside being top-notch fighters on medium tackle, bluefish are table fare supreme, at least when their dark, oily meat is eaten fresh, or smoked, or has been filleted and frozen by someone who understands what's needed. Bluefish are increasingly important to commercial fishermen too. Connoisseurs know how to identify fresh bluefish, in season, in the market; the rest of us buy and enjoy a flavorful fish called "Boston pollock."

It's all the same.

Bonefish

TO TAKE A BONEFISH on rod and reel has assumed the aura of climbing Mount McKinley, or winning the Bermuda Race, or achieving some other similar sporting milestone. The bonefish, "speedster of the flats," is so spooky it must be stalked like a deer, so ghostly translucent it can hardly be seen against a sandy bottom, so finicky few lures attract it, so fast few reel drags can tire it. Oh, come on now. If you want a bonefish, that can be arranged, almost without fail. Because, you see, they take a bait as readily as any fish— a juicy gob of crab, say, minus its shell, impaled on a hook, and left up for grabs on the bottom. In such clear water you'll be able to see the take, then leisurely announce your presence with a haul on the rod. The bonefish will indeed streak for the horizon, but if you're armed with fifteen-pound-test monofilament on a moderately long and strong rod, and a decent spinning or casting reel with a couple hundred yards capacity, you should have little trouble joining the supposedly elite fraternity who have notched up a bonefish.

Of course you can make it tougher, and for many sportsmen that's what it's all about. The challenge is not unlike tarpon fishing if you choose a fly rod. The basics are the same: a casting platform in the bow of a tiny, shallow-draft skiff; strong sunlight; a constant wind that always seems to come from just the wrong direction; and hours of staring at shifting patterns of sun and shadow on the water and the bottom. Since bonefish are truly translucent— you can actually see through their fins, for example— and, at two to fifteen or so pounds, far smaller than tarpon, the hardest part of bonefishing is simply locating the little rascals out in front of you. If you assign a week to catch your first bone, figure the first two or three days will be occupied simply in learning what shapes to look for in that kaleidoscope of light and dark. Your guide will point and gesticulate and shout and cajole, making you feel like a complete dunce, until suddenly you get the picture: *Oh, there it is.* And that's from the elevation of a boat; after a bit you can graduate to stalking them on foot, wading in knee-deep, blood-warm water, straining your eyes even more.

Polarizing sunglasses and a long-brim hat (with a dark underside) are as important as rod & reel to bonefishing, and even after you learn to spot them, countless times you'll be startled by bones streaking away almost from underfoot— you didn't see them and they eventually saw you.

Bonefish come with the advancing tide up onto shallow, marly coral flats, feeding up-sun and up-current with their heads down, scouring the bottom with their underslung mouths for crabs and snails. In very shallow water, their long, forked tails stick up into the air like waving seagrass. (When you're wading it's a good idea to squat periodically to scan the horizon for these tailing fish.) If the fish are moving toward you, stop. Wait. Cast your fly or jig toward the fish. If conditions are right you can simply let it settle to the bottom, then begin to strip line in when the fish is almost on top of it. But do it easy— anything that lives in such skinny water is very uptight about self-preservation. If all goes well, the bone will take note, then shoot after your offering, finally pouncing on it. All this is in plain view, of course, and it can be nerve-wracking. Many greenhorns (and pros) jump the strike and pull the hook away. Never mind your thundering pulse— wait till you feel the fish before ripping those lips.

Then it's off for the horizon, or at least the deeper water where bonefish retreat to. It doesn't seem possible, but an eight-pound bonefish, considered a fine catch, will peel upwards of a hundred yards of line off a reel within maybe ten seconds. A big one, if you let it, will clean you right out. You'll see bonefish anglers holding their rods way up over their heads when a fish runs. This is supposed to make the fish lift its head, and thus keep your line off the abrasive bottom and out of the coral. Well, if it makes you feel good, do it. But hanging on through that first run is largely a matter of luck. Then you crank it in. The fish will see you at some point; then it will make another, but shorter, mad dash. Again you crank it in. Again it sees you and runs. Three times should do it. Then the fish will turn sideways and circle your boat for a while, refusing to be brought closer. But they get tired, sometimes before you do, and do indeed

come in. Pictures, admiration. Bonefish taste pretty good, especially marinated in lemon, but they do deserve their name, and preparing them for the table is quite a job. Let it go.

Until recently, it was thought that bonefish were peculiar to the Gulf Coast, the Florida Keys, and the Caribbean, and those are still prime bonefish grounds. But then someone discovered that, hey, virtually every atoll in the Pacific Basin has all kinds of bonefish on its coral flats, and so does the north coast of South America. So while the bone is truly a desirable gamefish, it is not at all rare. Sight-fishing for them offers a level of excitement that is almost unique.

A bonefish of about eight pounds, the lower lobe of its tail rounded by foraging in the coral. Author's photograph.

115

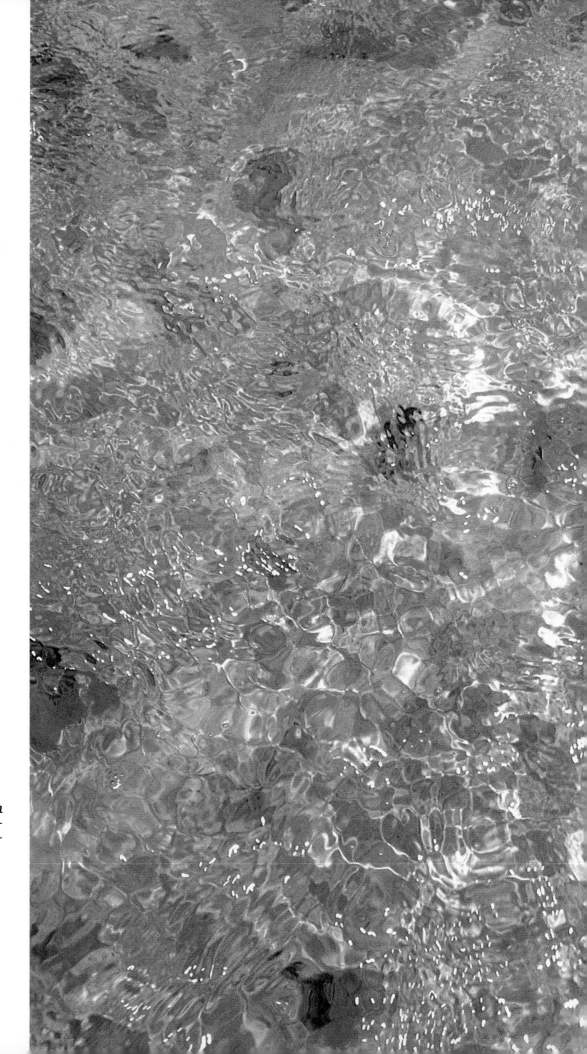

Masters of camouflage, bonefish seem virtually translucent to strong sunlight. R. Valentine Atkinson photograph.

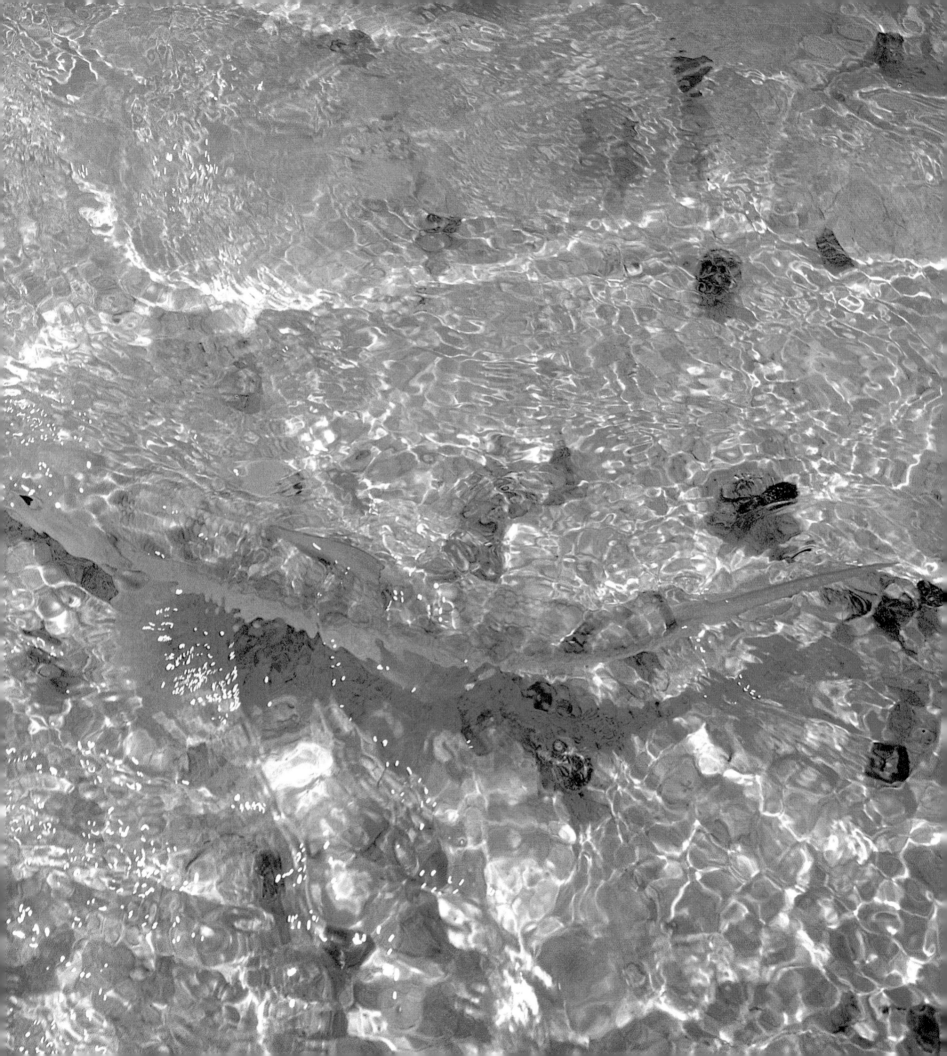

Bonito

ATLANTIC AND PACIFIC bonito are usually found offshore, and they are on the small side, for ocean fish, and so they are perhaps less sought than they deserve by sportfishermen. But the fortunate ones who hook into bonito when they do come inshore may vow to follow them to the ends of the earth— or the sea. If only in the hopes of eventually seeing one, for few light-tackle fishermen actually land their first bonito. In fact they wouldn't know just what it was that grabbed their lure and headed out for the open *right now* unless an experienced bonito fisherman, maybe standing next to them on the jetty, nodded sagaciously and said something like, "Yup, bonito all right. Speedy little devils."

At five to maybe fifteen pounds, the bonito looks like a small and slightly streamlined tuna, with that family's powerful sickle tail and the rows of little finlets behind the anal and dorsal fins. Bonito are distinctively barred, and the way these stripes rise gradually from the fish's midline toward its tail make the bonito look like it's doing thirty knots just sitting still. Bonefish are renowned speedsters, but I've caught many bones that could have taken swimming lessons from the average bonito. In hot pursuit of foodfish, bonito sometimes skip clear out of the water.

Besides being hard to hold onto, bonito are simply hard to hook, at least on light tackle. Their mouths are toothy, hard and strong, and they will

118

BONITO (Sarda sarda)

sometimes clamp onto a hook and bulldog it around for a while before simply opening their jaws and spitting it out; without a powerful rod, the fisherman can't always drive that hook point home.

Offshore, bonito school like bluefish, and often feed on the surface, so with persistence fishermen can track them down. Once a school shows itself, fish can be taken on almost any sort of gear, but until you reach that happy point, troll with cut baitfish or juicy strips of squid.

Dolphin

THE DOLPHIN has an identity problem only among people who've never seen one. All it takes is a glance at this unusual, Technicolor fish, and no one would ever confuse it with Flipper or any other porpoise. Dolphins have high, blunt foreheads, like cartoon whales, and an equally distinctive Mohawk-style dorsal fin that tapers evenly from the fish's brow almost to its tail. The body itself is a long, tapered wedge, flattish in cross-section, and ending in a V-shaped tail. All this makes dolphins, particularly the males with their fantastically square heads, appear to be natural-born wave-crashers, rowdy bruisers who don't always look before they leap.

And that's about how they behave for us fishermen. Dolphin are generally deep-water school fish, and their strength and predatory feeding behavior make them an offshore prize second only to billfish and big tuna. On the East Coast dolphins follow the warm waters of the Gulf Stream sometimes as far north as New England. Dolphin are widespread in the Pacific too; they're highly regarded as sporting table fare in Hawaii, where they appear on toney menus as *mahi-mahi.*

They're not hard to find and they're not easy to spook and they're not hard to fool, all of which makes dolphin a prime target for the headboats who take casual fishermen out for a day's trolling in the Gulf. Dolphin are surface feeders, attracted to any sort of debris floating on or in the water, and there are lots of stories about fantastic catches made alongside drifting tree trunks, ladders, hatch covers and so on. It doesn't matter much what sort of tackle you choose for dolphin so long as it's at least moderately heavy; the average fish caught on a hook is about ten to twenty pounds, and they fight hard enough. But there's always the possibility of a fifty-pounder, an encounter with which will leave you breathless and shaking. The strike alone may do you in— when three dolphin rush a bait at once, crashing over and through the water to converge on it like the Blue Thunder pursuit boats on a drug-runner, your pulse may redline even *before* they hit you.

A pacific dolphin struggles against the hook. Christine Fong photograph.

Multiple hookups aboard a dolphin partyboat. The man at the transom is fishing with a fly rod, unusual in such situations. R. Valentine Atkinson photograph.

Permit

Even a small permit is a large trophy for the saltwater fly fisherman. Linda Rogers took this photograph of her husband, Neal.

MANY FISHERMEN may think a permit is something the warden checks while they're fishing. But the **permit** alluded to in the section on bluegills is a fish, not a license—a silvery-green marvel of a gamefish that, while not rare, has nevertheless been taken by few anglers who do not use bait.

Permit are large pompano, with flat, powerful bodies, symmetrical anal and dorsal fins, and handsome, deeply forked tails. Like bonefish, permit are usually spotted in shallow, tropical waters over sandy bottoms, where they also grub for mollusks and crabs. But permit are warier and harder to approach, and while they do school, it's rare now in the Keys to see more than a dozen or so at once. The biggest ones—fifty-pounders have been subdued on rod and line, and larger ones reported—seem to be solitary creatures. Pound for pound, permit are even stronger swimmers than bonefish; though their dashes on the hook are usually shorter, they're more violent, and a permit will fight long, long after a bonefish would have tired. This extra strength makes it almost impossible to snub a big permit, to keep it up on the flat and away from the coral, sponges and sea grass where the fish wants to wrap your line up.

As if this weren't enough, a permit's shell-cracking mouth is extremely rubbery and strong, sometimes tough enough to crush a heavy saltwater hook. The fisherman who overcomes every adversity finally to get a "take" from a permit may find he can't seem to drive the hook point home no matter how often or how hard he strikes. The fish goes free because it spit the hook or the fisherman broke or weakened his own line. No fishing is more frustrating than permit fishing.

But it's not impossible. To catch a permit, set out especially for permit—don't futz around looking for bones or tarpon or whatever at the same time. (Unless you know the area, you'll need a guide.) When you finally spot a group of these dusky moonshapes, bait your medium spinning tackle with a live crab and ease on in. Feeding permit have their heads down and their minds in the sand; don't wince if your offering makes a gentle *plop* on the water, for that may get a fish's attention. If not, leave the bait on the bottom, let the school overswim it slightly, then draw attention to it with a tiny twitch of the rod. They are fickle; nothing you do may interest them in the least. If your patience is unusually saint-like and your skills and nerves are up to it, consider trying to join the handful of anglers who have successfully taken permit on fly tackle, from a skiff or on foot.

Whatever your *modus operandi*, keep three things in mind: First, your best hope is a school. Permit are competitive fish, and if two spot your lure at once, they may race each other to the attack. Second, be prepared to invest many hours and days in your first permit. And third, in no other fishing does luck play a greater part.

125

A large permit cruises the flats in search of crabs and other food. Lefty Kreh photograph.

Redfish

THE RED DRUM, or **redfish**, achieved fame recently on two fronts—cuisine and conservation. New Orleans chef Paul Prudhomme's Cajun recipe for "blackened redfish" swept the nation and appeared on every trendy menu from Boston to San Francisco. And the resultant commercial pressure on redfish stocks brought a great—and timely—hue and cry from Gulf Coast sportfishermen and fisheries biologists. The situation appears to be settling down, however, as the fad does what all fads do and passes away. (Although I did recently notice a dish called "Blackened Salmon" in a restaurant in Nome, Alaska, of all places.)

On the warmwater flats of the Gulf Coast from Texas to Florida Bay, fishermen routinely see redfish up to about ten pounds, sometimes in the open and sometimes right in the sea grass. They are handsome animals, dusky red with vertical tiger stripes on their backs and sides, and the slightly underslung mouths of fish who pluck food off the bottom. Unlike bonefish, however, reds will happily come to the surface for things like bass poppers. They also like streamers, however, similar to what you might offer a tarpon in the same region. Flats redfish are not electrifying fighters, but neither do they roll over and die on you. They are good eating, though, to their own misfortune.

In what seems almost a different incarnation, reds are a very important gamefish along the Eastern Seaboard, particularly in the spring and off the Carolina coast around Cape Hatteras. Here these fish grow huge—to fifty pounds or more—and they're known as channel bass. Anglers take them in much the same way stripers are caught farther up the coast, on everything from trolled lures to surf tackle to large streamer flies cast on 12-weight lines. The bass sometimes show up here in great schools that turn the sea red.

A large red drum comes ashore through the Outer Banks surf. Joel Arrington photograph.

128

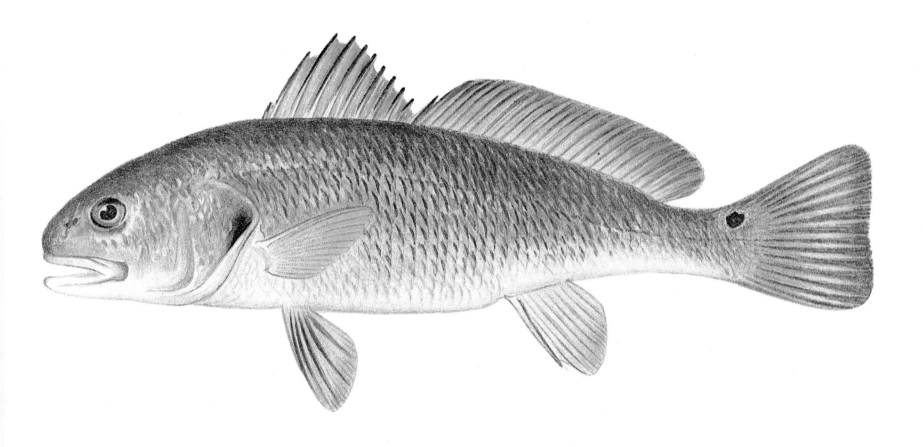

A table-size redfish, or channel bass.
Lefty Kreh photograph.

Sharks

SPORTFISHING FOR SHARKS became big business only when the *Jaws* movies awakened some bloodthirsty need in us to dominate this dreaded "maneater." Overnight, charterboat captains around the rim of the country (and in shark-infested regions such as Australia and South Africa) began offering shark-fishing excursions that often degenerated into savagery. Biologists, conservationists and clear-headed anglers—aware of the havoc this same blood lust had brought upon another victim of hysteria, the American wolf—began to crusade against the slaughter. Maybe it's worked; the frenzy appears to have died down. Or maybe it's just dormant, waiting for the next film.

Serious offshore fishermen everywhere have known all along that some sharks—makos, porbeagles, whites, tigers—are top-rank gamefish that give little away to the billfish and the bluefin tuna in size, speed, strength and the willingness to slug it out till hell freezes over. Big sharks have reportedly jumped thirty feet clear of the water when hooked, and every now and again a particularly hyperactive individual comes right aboard, under its own steam and considerably ahead of schedule. (Can you imagine the justifiable panic? The potential for injury and destruction?) What many people may not be aware of is that even light-tackle fans can enjoy shark fishing—near shore and without the expense associated with big-game trolling.

Thanks to their incredible sense of taste/smell and keen bioelectronic receptors, sharks are not hard to find, especially in warm waters. They may home in on a wounded fish already on your line (lots of sharks are hooked by fishermen who started out fishing, successfully, for something else) or respond to purposeful chumming with bloody baits. The problem with shark fishing is that the list of don'ts is a lot longer than the list of do's. Sharks bite, you see, even the little ones and the ones everyone agrees aren't prime maneaters. But that's an undeniable part of their appeal.

Marine biologists prepare to tag and release a blacktip shark. Douglas Perrine photograph.

Following spread:
Tiger Shark. Douglas Perrine photograph.

A lemon shark captured on a setline. Douglas Perrine photograph.

The first *don't* might be don't do it at all unless you're already a very experienced saltwater fisherman, or you go with someone who is. Here's another one— don't bring a hooked shark into your boat, again unless you or the crew know what you're doing and have some need to do so. Don't try to recover a lure, fly or bait from a shark's mouth, either, even with long disgorgers. Don't try to pick a small shark up in your hands— most are almost as flexible as snakes and much stronger, and if the teeth don't get you, the sandpaper hide can literally flay you. Sharks seem to be hard to kill, and sometimes they may be dead but they just don't know it yet. The jaws of a carcass riddled by shotgun blasts and whose spine was severed by slashes from a machete may suddenly snap shut an hour later. The convulsive thrashing of even a five-footer may break someone's leg or arm.

So leave your shark in the water, alive but tired, alongside the boat. No gaffs— the blood will draw other sharks. Take its picture, ooh and ahh over it, then snip the line (not too close, now) and re-rig. Let the fish have your lure; it likely won't even know it's there, and digestive acids plus salt water usually corrode a hook into nothingness in a matter of days. If you must kill a shark, tow it behind your boat by a tail-rope; it will drown quickly. Trying to shoot or bludgeon a shark from the often-slippery deck of a boat on a heaving sea can be more dangerous than the shark itself.

Fishermen looking for bonefish or any of the warmwater flats fish often encounter small sharks, and that's probably the best way to fish for sharks on purpose too. But while everyone who's ever poled the flats fruitlessly for hours succumbs to temptation and throws their tarpon streamer at a cruising blacktip, the ones who manage to bring a shark to hand are those who rigged up beforehand with wire tippets. (Some

136

fishermen leave a shark rod, ready to go, in the gunwale rack.) Sharks seem to go after any lure or fly big enough to catch their attention. But casting to a moving shark demands speed and accuracy — most sharks undulate along so gracefully that they seem to be moving slowly, yet in fact they're upon you and gone very quickly. And even a big shark that needs fear nothing will flinch away from a clumsy, splashy presentation. As you strip, strip your offering along, and the shark turns to chase, don't strike too soon— remember that its mouth is way down underneath its head, not out on the nose. Then simply hang on. If your hook point is surgically sharp and if it finds the right spot, along the lip or jaw, you may get lucky.

Shark fishing on the flats offers this advantage: You can spot the "push" in the water, see the fish, then gauge its size, and so assess the amount of trouble you're likely to get into on a successful hook-up. Most such sharks are well under six or seven feet long, and manageable. But much larger individuals— blues longer than your skiff, for example— sometimes come up into the shallows, especially during spawning. Although big-game fishermen scorn blues as pushovers, your chances of landing something like that on light tackle are virtually nil. Chumming sharks up from deeper water, whether off Cape Hatteras or the Baja, is usually not difficult, especially with the help of locals who know where to start, but you never know just what will take your offering. Often it will be a sixty- or seventy-pound mako (which is excellent eating, by the way), but then again. . . . It might be a cousin of the 3,427-pound great white shark that captains Donnie Braddick and Frank Mundus brought to the dock at Montauk, Long Island, on August 6, 1986.

The 3,427-pound great white shark taken by Captains Frank Mundus and Donnie Braddick off Montauk, New York, on August 6, 1986. Photograph courtesy of Berkley Line Co.

Snook

IT MAY BE personal bias, but I do believe that most of our truly exciting gamefish live in the tropical seas of Florida and the Gulf Coast. Some of them—tarpon, for example—come close to being household words even in nonsporting households. Others are less well-known but equally deserving. Such as the snook. I don't know where the name comes from, but I've been, ah, snookered by a number of these strong, cagy rascals.

Like many of their neighbor species, snook feed on crabs and shellfish, but they're also efficient (not to say spectacular) predators of the myriad free-swimming baitfish of warm waters. You may see snook busting up schools of smaller fish in a manner that would make a northern bluefish take notice. So snook have first-class teeth in that distictively underslung jaw. The rest of the fish is highly recognizable as well, from its tall double dorsals and humpbacked, vaguely pike-like silhouette to the bold black line that runs laterally down each flank. In the clear waters of the Gulf, the snook's racing stripe is very visible, especially against the silvery or bronze green of its body.

Bait and plug fishermen often do well on snook by night-fishing from Florida's saltwater bridges. The fish usually hang in the tide on the upcurrent side, sometimes near enough so they show up as dark shapes by the bridge lights. They may be in quiet hidey-holes, in the lee of the pilings, or near the shore, but they're waiting alertly for food to wash or swim by. If you're armed with medium-heavy spinning or casting tackle, by all means oblige them. Snook are tough customers.

But it's more interesting to stalk snook from a skiff, casting into sheltered areas and deep spots in the bays or tidal rivers if you can't jump them in the open. The best game of all is trying to pull snook out of their lairs in the mangroves. These are stillwater pockets, and even a small splash may spook snook, so fly tackle has an advantage here. A double advantage, in fact: By false-casting, a fly fisherman can gauge distance and direction, and line up the final cast just right before making his presentation. The fly has to go in deep, right back in among the snags. That's where the fish is. If everything goes well, you'll see your bright saltwater streamer very clearly as it begins to work—strip, strip, it's gone! Bang!

(Or maybe not; snook can be as temperamental as educated trout.)

If it's a snook of eight or ten pounds, and if you react quickly enough, and your leader knots are good, and your rod has enough backbone, you'll be able to snake the fish out of there. But you might have hooked a thirty-pounder, or contracted buck fever. Until you've witnessed it, you can't quite comprehend how quickly a snook can vanish back into the bushes, often snapping your tippet like string in the mangrove roots.

But sometimes you find snook in the open, or you win the battle of the bushes. Then it's on to the rest of the war. Snook are thrashers who don't give up easily, and their mouths are hard and abrasive. Experienced fly anglers rig up with a shock tippet of thirty- or forty-pound-test monofilament, and plug casters often use stainless-steel wire tippets for snook. These fish have a secret weapon, too—a section at the edge of each gill cover that's as sharp as a knife and parts line accordingly. Keep this cutter in mind when you're handling snook; fortunately they have jaws like largemouth bass and they are easy to "lip."

A seventeen-pound snook taken on a fly in Florida Bay. Lefty Kreh photograph.

A snook emerging from its lair under a coral head. Douglas Perrine photograph.

Striped Bass

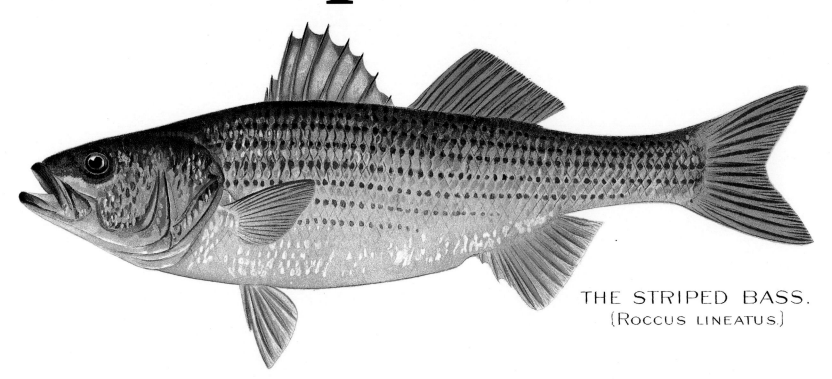

THE STRIPED BASS.
(Roccus lineatus.)

An East-Coast striped bass, caught at night. Lefty Kreh photograph.

ALONG WITH BEING an unusually desirable gamefish, the **striped bass** is just plain unusual, for it is now almost as popular with inland, freshwater anglers as it is with coastal fishermen. Taking a cue from striper spawning behavior, which draws them from the ocean up into the brackish estuaries of the Sacramento/San Joaquin, the Hudson, and other major rivers, and from the existence of more-or-less nonmigratory strains of bass that live in New York's St. Lawrence and Louisiana's Lake Ponchartrain systems, biologists began landlocking stripers in fresh water about twenty years ago. The experiment was such a success that now more than half our states offer such "impoundment striper" fishing. (There are, I'm told, new fishermen coming along who are surprised to learn that "their" lake stripers can also be caught in salt water.)

But along both coasts, it would be difficult to name a more important sport fish. It's a safe assumption that the boatload of fishermen trolling San Francisco Bay, or the lone caster slinging his pencil-body lure into the cold Oregon surf, or the group heading over the Cape Cod dunes in the beachbuggy with the rod rack on the bumper are after striped bass.

While these predatory bass can be caught on light tackle— and even fly rods when they're feeding along the inshore shallows of, say, Chesapeake Bay— classic striper fishing is off the beach. A lonely, windswept beach, preferably at night, with a strong tidal rip boiling around a bunch of rocks. In chest-high waders you struggle for balance as the waves break around you, winding up with arms and shoulders and torso to launch a heavy, aerodynamic lure as far out as your twelve-foot surf stick will reach. Feel the sting of the monofilament on your casting finger, hear the heavy whirr of line cascading off the spool of the big Penn, see it arching away into the night sky. Instinct and experience tell you when to brake, to control the line as the lure crashes down into the water unseen, maybe a hundred yards out. Then the retrieve— a fast, jigging dance through and on top of the sea. And if

you're lucky, a heart-stopping strike. Win or lose, as you trudge back for coffee at the driftwood fire above the tideline, you're already storing away a memory that will keep for years.

Stripers are wonderful eating, those few you decide to keep, offering flaky, white meat that tastes as good alone as it does with champagne sauce. And they are exceedingly handsome fish— nothing could be easier to recognize, with those horizontal pinstripes set against silvery sides and a greeny-black back. And, best of all, they get big. Huge, in fact. Sometimes fifty pounds and more of marine muscle that doesn't give up without a prolonged battle.

Those stripers who moved inland have, surprisingly, given up almost nothing in size and fight. The freshwater record, for example (caught in, of all places, the Colorado River in Arizona), is a few ounces under sixty pounds, and I'll guarantee that fish wasn't boated in ten minutes.

In salt water, the striper competes with other tough fish for the angler's attention, and it does so very well. But in most lakes, nothing comes even close to a striped bass as a potent combination of size, speed, strength, looks and a voracious appetite. In large impoundments stripers may be found almost anywhere, from the surface to several hundred feet down, feeding on almost anything that swims or crawls. Finding them is a matter of searching effectively, with long, water-covering casts near the sort of underwater structure that harbors baitfish. Lures or flies should thus imitate these forage fish in color, length, action (and also depth, of course). And your tackle better be of salmon/steelhead caliber— or heavier.

Particularly in southern states, the hard-fighting, one-foot-long, widebody "striper" you may find out in open lakes is likely a **white bass**, a native freshwater relative of the saltwater bass. And where both fish cohabit the same water, especially where there are good spawning grounds, you will almost certainly also find **whiterock bass**, which are female striper/male white hybrids. (In the South, striped bass are often called rockfish. And in Florida, the sunshine bass is a reverse hybrid— male striper, female white.) The hybrid is, not surprisingly, about midway between its parents in size, favoring the white side of the family in body proportions. Its chief distinction is that its stripes are irregular and broken, but it is also a fine gamefish that is now being stocked by itself.

A northern California striped bass. Christine Fong photograph.

144

WHITE BASS, (Roc

s Chrysops, Rafinesque.)

Tarpon

IT'S BEEN SAID before but it's worth saying again: if a world-class sportsman set out to design a world-class gamefish for fly tackle, he couldn't do better than the **tarpon**, the silver king. It grows to prodigious size, often hurles itself upon the fly as though it were candy, fights with the abandon of a sailor on shore leave, and does us the kindness of visiting shallow, warm waters where flies are most effective and where we can easily see the fish coming (and where we can also escape a northern winter).

It's difficult to capture the strength and agility of a tarpon in print; no matter how much you read, nothing quite prepares you for your first hookup with a big one. How big? In the Florida Keys, tarpon routinely exceed a hundred pounds, and six feet in length. A hundred and fifty isn't rare. The IGFA world record for fly rod is 188 pounds, and the all-tackle record is an almost unbelievable 283 pounds—a fish taken in Venezuela's Lake Maracaibo.

In the springtime, tarpon show up at the Keys, migrating—from no one knows quite where—to spawn in shallow estuaries. Anglers by the hundreds also come, for the thrill of their lives, standing on the tiny foredeck of a skiff for hours in the throbbing sun, prepared at a moment's notice to launch a huge streamer fly toward an oncoming fish. The guide watches from his poling platform, sometimes moving the boat, often anchoring in a pass between reefs or islands, waiting in ambush. Suddenly they're there—huge shapes in the shallow sea, dark against the white sand. The school is on you in no time; with shaking hands you drop your fly, roll-cast forward to launch it, then swing into the double-haul you practised at home for months. But here it doesn't go so smoothly—the wind is strong, from a bad direction. The sun is in your eyes, your hands are slippery with sweat, the line always finds something on the boat to coil around, the fish are just fifteen feet beyond your best-ever reach. And they're coming so fast, then going right by, and they are so big it's scary. *Omigawd, what if I really do hook one of those bastards?!*

If you really do, you'll be put to the test, you and your tackle. Because this is shallow water, the tarpon will have no place to go but sideways, or up. Lots of up. A giant tarpon may jump twenty times, as much as ten feet out of the water. It may run off three hundred yards of your line in a couple of eyeblinks, or it may choose to go airborne only a rod length from your gunwale. Tarpon have been known to jump right *into* a boat. (Or, more accurately, to be pulled into a boat by an inexperienced fisherman who leans hard on the fish while it's in the air right next door.) Fishermen have died battling tarpon.

After several hours of this, you may get lucky and boat the monster, by swimming it, exhausted, close enough for the guide to lip-gaff it. And if you think the fish is beat, check yourself out: You have a tremendous bruise in your gut from the rod butt, smashed fingers, dry, cracked lips, stubbed toes, maybe a sprained ankle, and arm, shoulder and back muscles that will quiver in pain for days. And who knows when your blood pressure will subside.

But gulping in the water alongside is the biggest fish you've likely ever seen—a wild-eyed, prehistoric-looking torpedo, sixty, seventy or a hundred inches of muscle, clad in gleaming silver scales as big and hard as plates. This is one of life's moments, like when you dropped that huge, thick-necked, black-backed white-tail buck a few years ago, and you looked down at him in the bloody snow and thought, in pride and sorrow, *What have I done . . ?* But this time it's different. The guide hoists the fish's head out long enough for pictures, then you both revive the creature by moving it so water flows through its gills. Soon its strength is returning, and when the tarpon wants to go, there's no holding it back.

So tarpon fishing can be serious sport. It can demand highly specialized, outrageously expensive tackle and techniques and preparations, and much time.

Friends of mine spend hundreds of hours and thousands of dollars annually prospecting the coasts of Africa and South America for undiscovered tarpon grounds. But there are other ways, too. Baby tarpon of up to about thirty pounds are common in Florida's rivermouths, canals and salt ponds, and they are high-voltage sport on any sort of gear. And all along the Gulf Coast you can find tarpon, especially smaller ones, willing to strike stillfished bait or trolled lures or streamers. Many fishermen might just rather hook several dozen twenty- to fifty-pound fish in a day than sweat and pray for just a crack at two or three (or maybe no) giants. Your choice.

A magnificent Florida tarpon that will be walked through the water until it recovers and may safely be released. Linda Rogers photograph.

149

Tunas

FOR THE DEDICATED fishermen who pursue them offshore, the seven different tuna in North American waters provide top-shelf sport on both light and heavy tackle. Tuna are members of the mackerel family, and so share many common characteristics and often look confusingly alike, but they cover an astonishing range of size. The little tunny barely attains twenty pounds; on the other end of the scale, the giant bluefin may exceed a thousand pounds and is a game animal of equal rank to the African elephant. Yet both are, pound for pound, among the hardest-swimming fish we Americans know.

Just about all the tunas are creatures of the open ocean, rarely found inshore except occasionally when a combination of warmer sea temperatures and current meanders brings a school within sight of the tip of a coastal promontory such as Cape Cod or certain Bahamian islands. Another exception is Nova Scotia's Canso Strait, where migrating bluefins travel almost within reach of shore. Tuna are worldwide fish, common off our Atlantic and Pacific shores, that gener-ally stay within temperate to subtropic zones and follow huge, yet-undeter-mined migratory patterns. They school in sometimes-fantastic numbers (one authority reports schools of 50,000 skipjack tuna; but usually the larger the individual fish, the smaller the groups—you'll never find even 500 bluefins together) and gang up like Biblical scourges on baitfish. Tuna often feed near the surface, pushing the panicked bait upwards as they attack from below, and so crowds of diving seabirds are often the first sign of "tuna on top."

In shape and proportion, tuna are quintessential *fish* pleasingly symmetrical along their lateral lines, broad-shouldered, with a steeply tapering head, a deeply forked sickle tail and purposeful-looking fins. They are dark on top, silvery along sides and belly. Even dead they can look vital, so strong and streamlined are they. School-children asked to draw a fish turn out tuna.

The deepwater **albacore** is likely the best-known tuna, as its name is plastered on millions of those seven-and-a-half-ounce cans, and it is probably also the most valuable American tuna, thanks again to all those little cans (and the fish's prime white meat). Albacore are excellent light-tackle gamefish. On the East Coast they are found sometimes as far north as New England, but the West Coast is a better albacore sport-fishery—most of the records are held by Californians. The IGFA lists a fish of about eighty-eight pounds as the all-tackle mark. Albacore have dark-yellow fins, and over-extended pectorals that reach as far back as behind the anal fin. The finlets (on the fish's back and belly behind the dorsal) and the tail alike are trimmed in white. The false albacore, or **little tunny**, is often much smaller (twenty pounds or less) and it has dark splotches on its belly and wavy markings on its upper-rear sides and back, bordered by the lateral line. And if you cut one open you'll immediately see another difference, one that saves the tunny from commercial netters—very dark meat.

The only other tuna that the Food & Drug Administration lets packers apply the white meat label to is the **blackfin**, so called because its finlets are entirely black, without the often-typical yellow edging. White meat or no, it's not an important commercial fish; blackfins rarely reach fifty pounds and are commonly found only on the Atlantic Coast south of New Jersey. But they are highly desirable gamefish and they "eat pretty well," as the saying goes.

Skipjack tuna are about the same size as blackfins, and in fact the two are often found together, at least in the Atlantic. But skipjacks are Pacific fish too, and on the West Coast they're moderately important to commercial seiners, who sell them as light-meat tuna. A local name for them is "watermelon tuna," for they are decorated with gently curved horizontal dark stripes across their silver bellies.

Blackfin tuna, photgraphed by Bill Barnes.

Following spread:
A giant bluefin tuna striking a mackerel. Photographed in St. Margaret's Bay, Nova Scotia, by Gilbert van Ryckevorsel.

A once-in-a-lifetime shot of a bluefin tuna leaping after a baitfish, photographed by Lionel Martinez.

Allison tuna were originally thought to be a separate genus, but biologists decided that they are in fact simply large **yellowfin** tuna, the most colorful branch of the family. Under a blue-black back, the fish's silver belly bears vertical rows of light spots or streaks, with a golden-yellow or sometimes a bright blue stripe from eye to tail. All the fins are also a dusky yellow, and the finlets are trimmed in black; the tail lacks the white trailing edge that many tuna have. Big yellowfins are particularly easy to identify because their spectacular, overextended dorsal and anal fins often reach more than halfway back to tail. They do get big, too—although most taken by sportsmen weigh less than a hundred pounds, yellowfins probably reach four hundred pounds. This, plus their light meat, makes them worthwhile for commercial longliners as well as purse seiners. **Bigeye** tuna are very close to yellowfin in size, markings, distribution and importance. The best way to distinguish the two casually is by

their fins—bigeyes lack the huge, graceful banners above and below that make yellowfins look like they've been bisected by parentheses.

Which brings us back to the **bluefin**, the largest tuna, which occurs widely in temperate and subtropical regions of the American Atlantic and Pacific (and elsewhere). Bluefins, particularly the giants, are highly migratory. Tagged fish have been known to cover 5,000 miles in 50 days, traversing the Atlantic Basin from the Bahamas to Norway, for example. Bluefins come in all sorts of sizes, but all have short pectoral fins and their anal fin and finlets are dark yellow edged in black. They are fast-growing fish, capable of reaching close to seven hundred pounds in fourteen years. This spectacular growth means predatory feeding habits that are equally spectacular, and all the power, speed and aggressiveness that in turn calls for. All this is by way of putting the bluefin at the top of the tuna-angling heap both commercially and recreationally.

The two can be difficult to separate. Sportfishermen sometimes earn thousands of dollars in a single weekend by selling their fresh bluefin right on the dock. Buyers for the Japanese market hang around bluefin piers, bidding frantically for the hundreds of pounds of dark red meat that is so valuable for *sashimi* and *sushi*. Conservationists fear that the giant tuna are endangered, and in fact catches have declined drastically in some regions where big bluefins were once common.

For the chance at a thousand-pounder, the sportsman should go to the extreme tip of the bluefin's range. Only the largest, best-insulated tuna can survive the food-rich but chilled waters of Maritime Canada, for example, and such angling truly becomes big-game hunting. Supremely fast, strong, almost arrogant-seeming, the giant bluefin is all but invincible. To watch one of these creatures boil up from the depths and slash at a daisy chain of trolled bait is to be put firmly into one's proper puny place on the planetary scale. A successful hook-up means hours and hours of dogged concentration and teamwork between angler and boat captain and mate. One ill-considered move by any of them can part even 130-pound-test line instantly.

Most of us will never know the bittersweet elation of such combat, but we can still take tuna, even bluefin, on rod and line. The smaller types and individuals are often easy to find—in the right water and season—within a few hours' running time of our East and West coasts. Tunas readily strike natural baits such as squid or mackerel, and also big spoons or plugs. Once you've located a school, by trolling or chumming or both, even fly fishing becomes practical. Well, almost. A thirty-pound tuna hooked in the open sea, where it can dive deep as well as run, puts tremendous strain on light tackle. And a fifty-pound tuna is a fly fisherman's trophy of a lifetime.

A characteristically marked yellowfin tuna. Joel Arrington photograph.

Weakfish

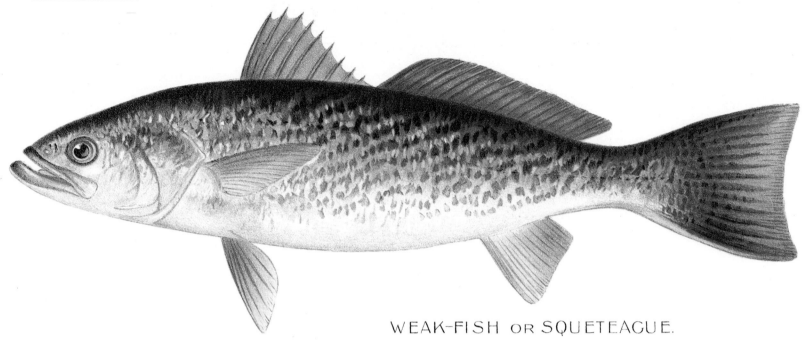

WEAK-FISH or SQUETEAGUE.
(CYNOSCION REGALE)

ITS NAME REFERS to the soft, easily torn tissues of its mouth; the **weakfish** is actually a strong gamefish, a fine, delicately fleshed table fish, and an indicator of environmental conditions. You may know it as the seatrout, or tiderunner. It covers the Atlantic Coast from Florida to New England, moving seasonally south or north to follow warmer temperatures. Except for its dorsal fins, it does generally resemble a trout, with handsome, if subdued, tones of green and blue over silver or bronze. Weakfish are also irregularly spotted on back and sides. Its projecting lower jaw is distinctly un-troutlike, however, and the upper jaw sports a pair of nasty canines.

The teeth are a clue; weakfish are predators, and not very choosy at that. They're opportunists that school up to chase herring, menhaden and any other baitfish, and they're not above crunching up shrimp, crabs and the like either. As fishermen, we have a host of baits and lures to choose from in tackling weakfish; the challenge (as always in the broad ocean) is locating them. In the warmer months they can be found in estuaries and the inshore shallows;

when the waters cool down they may go deeper. Weakfish can be caught from piers and jetties; from boats anchored where tidal flow moves food around; by trolling alongshore and through coves and rivermouths; and even in the surf. Because of their tendency to come to the top (and maybe because of the "trout" label), saltwater fly fishermen regard weaks as prime targets, and they put up a respectable battle on midweight tackle. And also like trout, weakfish seem to prefer cleaner, quieter waters. I'll always remember one brilliant dawn when our cruising boat was anchored in a little backwater of the Connecticut River estuary. There were so many weakfish feeding around us that their rolling and splashing woke me up, and I had plenty of time to ease over the side into the dinghy with my fly rod. For an hour the world was mine, shared only with the school of willing fish, a pair of feeding bald eagles (perhaps the reason no gulls came wheeling and screaming overhead), and the swiftly rising sun that coated everything with gold.

Although it's often regarded as the same fish, along the southern Atlantic Coast swims a cousin of the weakfish

A weakfish, or gray trout (left), and a speckled sea trout. Joel Arrington photograph.

Weakfish, photographed by Joel Arrington.

known as the **spotted seatrout**. It's very popular with anglers of Florida and the Gulf states. About the only way to differentiate it from the weakfish is by its spots—on the seatrout, the spots generally extend up onto the second dorsal fin and the tail—and its overall color. Seatrout seem to be brighter and more vividly marked (often a characteristic of tropical and semi-tropical fish) than the more northern weakfish. The feeding and breeding habits of both fish are much the same, and so fishing for them is very similar also. In the clear, warm waters from Florida to Texas, however, spotting seatrout is often easy, and this makes them a prime target for fly casters and light-tackle enthusiasts who prefer to stalk sighted fish. Like the weakfish, spotted seatrout are gourmet eating, offering a delicate white flesh that can all too easily be overcome by improper cooking or storage. They tend to run a bit smaller than weaks, however; they rarely grow bigger than ten or twelve pounds, while weakfish may run five pounds heavier.

Index

World Records

THE INTERNATIONAL GAME FISH Association, headquartered in Florida, is a nonprofit organization that has taken on the responsibility of vetting and keeping sportfishing records from around the world. It is also a powerful voice for fisheries conservation. It is not alone in the world in keeping such records, but it is the most respected of those groups, and it has officially designated representatives in virtually all the fishing corners of the world, no matter how remote. The records listed here are only for the fish mentioned in this book; the IGFA maintains data on many other species as well. For each fish there is an all-tackle record, which is the largest documented example of that species known to the IGFA; a group of line class records, that encompass fishing done with braided or monofilamentous lines (such as trolling, spincasting, baitfishing and so on); and then records for fish taken on fly tackle. Into which category a particular fish falls is determined by the breaking strain of the line or leader tippet it was caught on. The IGFA demands to see the actual line and hook a fish was taken with so that their lab may test it for actual tensile strength and also determine whether the rig meets their strict specifications for lengths, knots and so on.

The IGFA certification committee also naturally insists that record-contender fish be weighed on accurate scales. Most saltwater fishing marinas are equipped with such machinery. Anglers who fish in lakes and rivers, particularly in the bush where a government-certified grocery-story scale is not available nearby, may use hand-held scales. But these must have been checked by the IGFA both before and after a fish is taken. The length and girth of a fish must also be recorded, and the IGFA wants to see photographs and the signatures of witnesses as well. If you're interested in competing for a spot in the record book, which is updated annually, contact the Association at 3000 East Las Olas Boulevard, Ft. Lauderdale, Florida 33316 for information. Many anglers carry with them a small kit of materials and information, as well as an entry form, to help them conform to the IGFA's requirements upon landing a large fish. It is no longer

necessary, in these enlightened times, to kill all but the largest trophy fish in order to qualify for a record.

The fly rod records only go up to the 8-kilogram, or 16-pound, tippet level because the fly line itself, above the tippet and the leader, has a breaking strain of approximately that itself, and so there is little point to fishing with a heavier tippet. This also explains why so many fly rod records, particularly in salt water, are substantially lower than line-class records—there is simply no way to boat a 500-pound tuna on a 16-pound leader tippet, barring incredible applications of time, money, perseverance and even more plain old luck.

Reading the records is not as dry as it might seem, for trends and imagined situations become obvious. Certain names pop up over and over—record hunters whose skill or motivation or personal wealth (or all three) let them pursue a dream all over North America or even the globe. It is still possible to identify certain species who are "under-recorded," where line classes are still vacant or the existing marks can easily be broken, especially if you know where in the world to go. Many fishermen plan their annual vacations around a trip to a certain lake or river or bay, where for a week or two they will singlemindedly try to better a certain mark. If they are successful, they change to another line or tippet class and go at it again. This was aided and abetted recently by one of the line manufacturers, who offered, for some years, $1,000 for each and every IGFA record set on their line. They never dreamed how successful this promotion would be, and ended up awarding more than $1 million to fishermen around the world. Some skillful and successful anglers earned very comfortable annual wages for several years simply by fishing hard (and smart) with Berkley Trilene.

Note that the largest examples of many species, particularly the freshwater and smaller saltwater fish, have been taken on middle-level line weights. This is partly because records are often simply a matter of luck, and partly because the great majority of non-record-hunting fishermen fish with mid-level tackle. They're not out to prove anything, just have a good time. Statisti-

cally, then, this large group has a better chance of striking gold. In many cases, as you progress to the heavier line classes, the size of the record actually diminishes. Often these fishermen are specifically looking for a record, and luck simply doesn't go their way—another manifestation of the old law that says the harder you try, the behinder you get. And only you can decide how glorious it is to hold the 12-pound record for bluegill sunfish. Many exceptions are found in the big-game species, the fish that approach the ton mark. It's difficult enough to boat such a creature on 130-pound line, and sizes usually increase with each line class.

No one will ever know how many record fish have been caught and not recorded—released unknowingly, or caught on tackle that doesn't meet IGFA specifications, or simply taken home and eaten! And many expert fishermen have caught record-breakers and chosen not to enter them to the IGFA—because of inconvenience or the desire not to kill or stress a fish or even because they simply don't want their name in print.

BASS Largemouth (*Micropterus salmoides*)
22 lbs 4 oz/10.09 kg   Montgomery Lake, Georgia 2 June 1932   George W. Perry

Line Class
1 kg (2 lb)   11 lbs/5.00 kg   Lake Casitas, California   25 May 1982   Frank Gasperov, Jr.
2 kg (4 lb)   14 lbs 4 oz/6.46 kg   Cachuma Lake, California   8 May 1985   Clint Johanson
4 kg (8 lb)   21 lbs 3 oz/9.61 kg   Oakview, California   4 March 1980   Raymond D. Easley
6 kg (12 lb)   18 lbs 8 oz/8.39 kg   Lake Isabella, California   6 January 1985   Chris Moore
8 kg (16 lb)   17 lbs 4 oz/7.82 kg   Polk County, Florida   6 July 1986   McArthur Bill O'Berry
10 kg (20 lb)   17 lbs 12 oz/8.05 kg   Lake Tohopekaliga, Florida   11 July 1986   John Q. Faircloth

Fly Rod - Tippet Class
1 kg (2 lb)   7 lbs 9 oz/3.43 kg   Arivaca lake, Arizona   17 March 1984   Corky Dufek
2 kg (4 lb)   6 lbs 7 oz/2.92 kg   Lake Tsala, Florida   15 June 1977   Terry G. Warson
4 kg (8 lb)   13 lbs 9 oz/6.15 kg   Lake Morena, California   4 April 1984   Ned S. Sewell
6 kg (12 lb)   12 lbs 9 oz/5.70 kg   Lake Tsala, Florida   25 March 1984   Robert M. Ekker
8 kg (16 lb)   11 lbs 2 oz/5.04 kg   Lake George, Florida   8 April 1978

BASS: Smallmouth (*Micropterus dolomieui*)
11 lbs 15 oz/5.41 kg   Dale Hollow Lake, Kentucky   9 July 1955   David L. Hayes

Line Class
1 kg (2 lb)   5 lbs 13 oz/2.63 kg   James River, Richmond, Virginia   20 March 1985   Robert H. Blevins

2 kg (4 lb)   6 lbs 13 oz/3.09 kg   Pickwick lake, Alabama   22 February 1983   Michael A. Curry
4 kg (8 lb)   10 lbs 8 oz/4.76 kg   Hendricks Creek, Kentucky   14 April 1986   Paul E. Beal
6 kg (12 lb)   8 lbs 8 oz/3.85 kg   Watts Bar Lake, Tennessee   6 April 1984   Lenny Cecil
8 kg (16 lb)   7 lbs 6 oz/3.34 kg   Tennessee River, Alabama   5 March 1986   Charles L. Tibbs

Fly Rod - Tippet Class

1 kg (2 lb)   2 lbs 3 oz/0.99 kg   George Lake, Manitoba, Canada   17 July 1983   James H. Miller
2 kg (4 lb)   4 lbs 1 oz/1.85 kg   Titus lake, New York   13 July 1985   Ronald D. Parl
4 kg (8 lb)   3 lbs 13 oz/1.72 kg   E. Grand Lake, N.B., Canada   16 May 1984   Bill White
4 kg (8 lb)   TIE   3 lbs 14 oz/1.78 kg   Ft. Loudon Lake, Tennessee   9 June 1984   Jean H. Leidersdorf
6 kg (12 lb)   4 lbs 6 oz/1.98 kg   James River, Virginia   4 September 1985   Noel Burkhead
8 kg (16 lb)   1 lb 9 ox/0.70 kg   Flaming Gorge Reservoir, Utah   20 September 1985   Ray Johnson

BASS: Striped, landlocked (Morone saxatilis)   59 lbs. 12 oz./27.10 kg.   Colorado River, Arizona   26 May 1977   Frank W. Smith

Line Class

1 kg (2 lb)   21 lbs 4 oz/9.63 kg   Savannah River, Georgia   15 July 1984   Stephen Bayazes
2 kg (4 lb)   38 lbs 12 oz/17.57 kg   Lake Norfork, Arkansas   9 February 1983   Bryce Frits, Jr.
4 kg (8 lb)   45 lbs 8 oz/20.63 kg   Lake Cumberland, Kentucky   18 April 1978   Walter C. Lilly
6 kg (12 lb)   47 lbs/21.31 kg   Flint River, Georgia   23 March 1983   Garry Whitehead
8 kg (16 lb)   59 lbs 12 oz/27.10 kg   Colorado River, Arizona   26 May 1977   Frank W. Smith
10 kg (20 lb)   52 lbs 8 oz/23.81 kg   Colorado River, Arizona   27 June 1976   Robert G. Stahl
15 kg (30 lb)   47 lbs 11 oz/21.64 kg   Flint River, Georgia   7 March 1986   Don Allen Fowler
24 kg (50 lb)   48 lbs 5 oz/21.91 kg   Flint River, Georgia   20 May 1983   John Hoffpauir, Jr.

Fly Rod - Tippet Class

1 kg (2 lb)   19 lbs 4 oz/8.73 kg   All American Canal, California   15 May 1982   Dr. Edward J. Cramer
2 kg (4 lb)   VACANT
4 kg (8 lb)   11 lbs 4 oz/5.10 kg   San Antonia Lake, California   18 October 1983   Roy Lawson
6 kg (12 lb)   9 lbs 8 oz/4.30 kg   Lake Havasu, California   15 July 1981   Paul lawson
8 kg (16 lb)   19 lbs 15 oz/9.06 kg   Silverwood lake, California   17 July 1986   Terry A. Baird
The four heavier classes appear to be ripe for the plucking—landlocked stripers grow to increasingly enormous sizes as their range widens (as the line class records indicate), and the relatively tiny fly rod marks likely indicate that the right angler has not yet found one of the monsters close enough to the surface for a good fly presentation. That day can't be far off, however.

BASS: White (Morone chrysops)   5 lbs 14 oz/2.66 kg   Kerr Lake, North Carolina   15 March 1986   Jim King

Line Class

1 kg (2 lb)   3 lbs 4 oz/1.47 kg   Devils Lake, North Dakota   29 December 1985   Matthew J. Cummings
2kg (4 lb)   5 lbs 6 oz/2.43 kg   Grenada, Mississippi   21 April 1979   W.C. Mulvihill

4 kg (8 lb)   5 lbs 9 oz/2.52 kg   Colorado River, Texas   31 March 1977   David S. Cordill
6 kg (12 lb)   4 lbs 3 oz/1.89 kg   Frisco, Texas   24 February 1984   Geoff Cross

Fly Rod - Tippet Class

1 kg (2 lb)   2 lbs 9 oz/1.18 kg   Pomme de Terre River, Minnesota   20 May 1982   R.E. Massey
2 kg (4 lb)   2 lbs 9 oz/1.17 kg   Lake Nacimiento, California   12 March 1983   Butch Olson
4 kg (8 lb)   3 lbs 8 oz/1.58 kg   Nacimiento River, California   6 March 1981   Cory Wells
6 kg (12 lb)   VACANT
8 kg (16 lb)   VACANT

BLUEGILL: (Lepomis macrochirus)   4 lbs 12 oz/ 2.15 kg   Ketona Lake, Alabama   9 April 1950   T.S. Hudson

Line Class

1 kg (2 lb)   1 lb 8 oz/0.70 kg   Pine Mountain, Georgia   14 May 1986   Stephen King
2 kg (4 lb)   2 lbs 12 oz/1.24 kg   Vaughn, Michigan   30 June 1983   Gary Saylor
4 kg (8 lb)   1 lb 14 oz/0.86 kg   Page County, Iowa   12 May 1985   Will T. Knoll
6 kg (12 lb)   4 lbs 3 oz/1.89 kg   Hopkins County, Kentucky   5 August 1980   Phil M. Conyers

Fly Rod - Tppet Class

1 kg (2 lb)   1 lb 4 oz/0.56 kg   Glendale Reservoir, Idaho   9 August 1984   Jim Dougherty
2 kg (4 lb)   1 lb 13 oz/0.83 kg   Colorado Springs, Colorado   14 May 1986   Raymond C. Sapp
4 kg (8 lb)   2 lbs 12 oz/1.25 kg   Guilford County, North Carolina   4 November 1984   Curtis R. Holmes, Jr.
6 kg (12 lb)   VACANT
8 kg (16 lb)   VACANT

BULLHEAD: black (Ictalurus melas)   8 lbs/ 3.62 kg   Lake Waccabuc, New York   1 August 1951   Kani Evans

Line Class

1 kg (2 lb)   2 lbs 13 oz/1.28 kg   Washington, Iowa   26 May 1985   Richard Greiner
2 kg (4 lb)   1 lb 15 oz/0.87 kg   Andrew County, Missouri   31 March 1984   Larry Lowdon
4 kg (8 lb)   6 lbs 9 oz/2.99 kg   Cowley County, Kansas   14 April 1985   Lyle J. Houghton
6 kg (12 lb)   7 lbs 5 oz/3.32 kg   Havana, Kansas   13 May 1985   David A. Tremain

Fly Rod - Tippet Class

All fly rod classes are VACANT

BULLHEAD: brown (Ictalurus nebulosus)   5 lbs 8 oz/2.49 kg   Veal Pond, Georgia   22 May 1975   Jimmy Andrews

Line Class

1 kg (2 lb)   2 lbs 4 oz/1.03 kg   Lake Beauclaire, Florida   15 January 1986   Roger Meyer
2 kg (4 lb)   3 lbs 14 oz/1.32 kg   Mountain Creek Lake, Georgia   26 February 1985   Stephen King
4 kg (8 lb)   3 lbs 13 oz/1.74 kg   Montgomery County, Alabama   8 April 1984   Charles A. Lane
6 kg (12 lb)   5 lbs 8 oz/2.49 kg   Veal Pond, Georgia   22 May 1975   Jimmy Andrews

Fly Rod - Tippet Class

All fly rod classes are VACANT

CATFISH: blue (Ictalurus furcatus)   97 lbs/ 43.99 kg   Missouri River. South Dakota   16 September 1959   Edward B. Elliott

Line Class

1 kg (2 lb)   4 lbs/1.81 kg   Kinston, North Carolina   7 July 1984   Debra Kay Crews
2 kg (4 lb)   27 lbs 1 oz/12.21 kg   Haakon County Lakes, South Dakota   29 April 1976   O.R. (Bob) Brancel
4 kg (8 lb)   58 lbs 8 oz/26.53 kg   Irvine Lake, California   6 July 1986   Glenn E. Bell

6 kg (12 lb)   67 lbs 14 oz/30.79 kg   Lake Texoma, Texas   12 November 1985   Nonnie Ledbetter
8 kg (16 lb)   81 lbs/36.74 kg   Kentucky Lake, Kentucky   22 June 1986   Dana A. Ballard
10 kg (20 lb)   79 lbs/35.83 kg   Lake Texoma, Oklahoma   14 May 1984   Viola McNabb
15 kg (30 lb)   81 lbs/36.74 kg   Washita River, Oklahoma   19 July 1985   Jerry G. Buchanan
24 kg (50 lb)   69 lbs/31.29 kg   Lake Texoma, Oklahoma   28 November 1980   W.H. Kirk
37 kg (80 lb)   80 lbs/36.28 kg   Lake Texoma, Oklahoma   28 November 1980   Ron J. Smith
60 kg (130 lb)   12 lbs 9 oz/5.69 kg   Kentucky Dam, Tennessee   19 June 1985   Teddy R. Coleman

Fly Rod - Tippet Class

All fly rod classes are VACANT

CATFISH: channel (Ictalurus punctatus)   58 lbs/26.30 kg   Santee-Cooper Reservoir, South Carolina   7 July 1964   W.B. Whaley

Line Class

1 kg (2 lb)   20 lbs 6 oz/9.27 kg   Red River, Manitoba   28 August 1985   Jeff C. Suggitt
2 kg (4 lb)   22 lbs 1 oz/10 kg   Red River, Manitoba   30 June 1986   Lamont M. Wegner
4 kg (8 lb)   37 lbs 6 oz/16.95 kg   Sebastian River, Florida   16 January 1983   Max D. Nowotne
6 kg (12 lb)   32 lbs 3 oz/14.61 kg   Satilla River, Georgia   30 October 1977   James I. Lentz
8 kg (16 lb)   41 lbs 8 oz/18.82 kg   Snake River, Nebraska   26 July 1985   Johnnie F. Cunning
10 kg (20 lb)   41 lbs/18.59 kg   Dunlap, Tennessee   30 July 1982   Clint Walters, Jr.
15 kg (30 lb)   41 lbs 8 oz/18.82 kg   Snake River, Nebraska   11 August 1986   Heather Jo Cunning
24 kg (50 lb)   33 lbs/14.96 kg   Snake River, Nebraska   15 August 1986   Johnnie F. Cunning
37 kg (80 lb)   25 lbs 2 oz/11.39 kg   Red River, Manitoba   2 August 1986   Rodney D. Adams

Fly Rod - Tippet Class

1 kg (2 lb)   1 lb 3 oz/0.54 kg   Coosa County, Alabama   28 June 1986   Vance H. Baker
2 kg (4 lb)   7 lbs/3.17 kg   Kinston, North Carolina   21 May 1984   Thomas E. Crews
4 kg (8 lb)   1 lb 1 oz/0.49 kg   Goose Creek, Virginia   6 August 1983   Rochlyn L. Lorey, Sr.
6 kg (12 lb)   2 lbs 15 oz/1.34 kg   Coosa County, Alabama   30 June 1986   Vance H. Baker
8 kg (16 lb)   9 lbs/4.08 kg   Lake Washington, Florida   15 March 1985   Robert C. Newby

CATFISH: flathead (Ictalurus olivaris)   98 lbs/ 44.45 kg   Lewisville, Texas   2 June 1986   William O. Stephens

Line Class

1 kg (2 lb)   30 lbs 1 oz/13.63 kg   St. Croix River, Minnesota   8 August 1986   Floyd F. Michlitsch
2 kg (4 lb)   49 lbs 8 oz/22.45 kg   Grays Lake, Iowa   1 July 1986   Pat Brady
4 kg (8 lb)   54 lbs/24.49 kg   Watts Bar Lake, Tennessee   30 June 1984   Eddie L. Rogers
4 kg (8 lb)   Tie   54 lbs/24.49 kg   Francis Case Reservoir, South Dakota   4 July 1986   Martin K. Horley
6 kg (12 lb)   91 lbs 4 oz/41.39 kg   Lake Lewisville, Texas   28 March 1982   Mike Rogers
8 kg (16 lb)   55 lbs/24.94 kg   thomas Hill Lake, Missouri   26 April 1986   Mark Lynn Epperson
10 kg (20 lb)   64 lbs 2 oz/29.08 kg   St. Croix River, Wisconsin   20 August 1985   Dave Olson
15 kg (30 lb)   98 lbs/44.45 kg   Lewisville, Texas   2 June 1986   William O. Stephens
24 kg (50 lb)   57 lbs 4 oz/25.96 kg   Colorado River, Arizona   16 April 1985   Mike Hughes
37 kg (80 lb)   34 lbs 8 oz/15.64 kg   St. Croix

River, Minnesota 22 August 1985 Joel M. Anderson
60 lbs (130 lb) 41 lbs 7 oz/18.79 kg St. Croix River, Minnesota 2 September 1985 Floyd F. Michlitsch
Fly Rod - Tippet Class
All fly rod classes are VACANT

CHAR: arctic (*Salvelinus alpinus*) 32 lbs 9 oz/ 14.77 kg Tree River, Northwest Territories 30 July 1981 Jeffery L. Ward
Line Class
1 kg (2 lb) 17 lbs 4 oz/7.82 kg Kugaryak River, Northwest Territories 26 August 1981 Raymond Goodrich
2 kg (4 lb) 21 lbs/9.52 kg Kugaryuk River, Northwest Territories 26 August 1981 Raymond Goodrich
4 kg (8 lb) 22 lbs 8 oz/10.20 kg Kugaryuk River, Northwest Territories 28 August 1978 Ruby A. Goodrich
6 kg (12 lb) 25 lbs/11.34 kg Kugaryuk River, Northwest Territories 28 August 1978 Raymond Goodrich
8 kg (16 lb) 28 lbs/12.70 kg Tree River, Northwest Territories 21 August 1985 Robert J. Frost, MD
10 kg (20 lb) 24 lbs/10.88 kg Victoria Island, Northwest Territories 30 July 1985 Chuck McCauley
15 kg (30 lb) 21 lbs 8 oz/9.75 kg Victoria Island, Northwest Territories 1 August 1981 Robert W. Kitchen
Fly Rod - Tippet Class
1 kg (2 lb) 6 lbs 12 oz/3.06 kg Basset Brook, Labrador 1 September 1983 Franklin F. Webb
2 kg (4 lb) 11 lbs/4.98 kg Coppermine River, Northwest Territories 4 July 1985 Thomas M. Bruno
4 kg (8 lb) 18 lbs 2 oz/8.22 kg Victoria Island, Northwest Territories 25 July 1981 Elmer M. Rusten
6 kg (12 lb) 15 lbs/6.80 kg Victoria Island, Northwest Territories 2 September 1980 Elmer M. Rusten
8 kg (16 lb) 14 lbs 12 oz/6.69 kg Kugaryuak River, Northwest Territories 14 August 1984 Jim Dixon

CRAPPIE: black (*Pomoxis nigromaculatus*) 4 lbs 8 oz/2.05 kg Kerr Lake, Virginia 1 March 1981 L. Carl Herring, Jr.
Line Class
1 kg (2 lb) 3 lbs 2 oz/1.44 kg Chickahominy Lake, Virginia 10 August 1986 Max Tongier, Jr.
2 kg (4 lb) 4 lbs 4 oz/1.92 kg Beaver Dam Lake, North Carolina 25 March 1984 Chris Ransom
4 kg (8 lb) 4 lbs 8 oz/2.05 kg Kerr Lake, Virginia 1 March 1981 L. Carl Herring, Jr.
6 kg (12 lb) 4 lbs 4 oz/1.92 kg Paint Creek, Alabama 18 March 1984 Sherril S. Harris
Fly Rod - Tippet Class
1 kg (2 lb) 2 lbs 3 oz/1.01 kg Lee Hall Reservoir, Virginia 20 March 1985 Max Tongier
2 kg (4 lb) 1 lb 9 oz/0.73 kg Carlisle County, Kentucky 11 May 1986 Allen Beard
4 kg (8 lb) 2 lbs 6 oz/1.07 kg Lee Hall Reservoir, Virginia 21 March 1985 Max Tongier
6 kg (12 lb) VACANT
8 kg (16 lb) VACANT

CRAPPIE: white (*Pomoxis annularis*) 5 lbs 3 oz/ 2.35 kg Enid Dam, Mississippi 31 July 1957 Fred L. Bright
Line Class
1 kg (2 lb) 2 lbs 11 oz/1.21 kg Delaware River, Pennsylvania 3 May 1986 Patricia Phillips
1 kg (2 lb) Tie 2 lbs 11 oz/1.21 kg Beaver Dam Lake, North Carolina 25 March 1984

Chris Ransom
2 kg (4 lb) 3 lbs/1.36 kg Delaware River, Pennsylvania 21 April 1985 John J. Phillips, Jr.
4 kg (8 lb) 3 lbs 12 oz/1.70 kg Alabama River, Alabama 31 March 1982 James E. Black
6 kg (12 lb) 4 lbs/1.81 kg Rome, Georgia 19 March 1980 Ken Wright
Fly Rod - Tippet Class
2 kg (4 lb) 2 lbs 8 oz/1.13 kg Amelia County, Virginia 6 September 1986 Adam S. Plotkin
All other fly rod classes are VACANT

DOLLY VARDEN: (*Salvelinus malma*) 10 lbs 2 oz/ 4.59 kg Kenai River, Alaska 31 August 1986 Ronald G. Reeves, Jr.
Line Class
1 kg (2 lb) 4 lbs 9 oz/2.09 kg Quigmy River, Alaska 5 July 1986 Terry Chase
2 kg (4 lb) 5 lbs 12 oz/2.62 kg Rocky River, Alaska 14 July 1986 Martin Vanderploeg
4 kg (8 lb) 8 lbs 1 oz/3.66 kg Nakwasina River, Alaska 14 July 1985 Loyal J. Johnson
6 kg (12 lb) 10 lbs 2 oz/4.59 kg Kenai River, Alaska 31 August 1986 Ronald G. Reeves, Jr.
Fly Rod - Tippet Class
1 kg (2 lb) 4 lbs 12 oz/2.15 kg Painter Creek, Alaska 23 September 1985 Burton R. Leed
2 kg (4 lb) 5 lbs 4 oz/2.38 kg Painter Creek, Alaska 27 September 1985 Burton R. Leed
4 kg (8 lb) 4 lbs 8 oz/2.04 kg Painter Creek, Alaska 24 September 1985 Burton R. Leed
6 kg (12 lb) 8 lbs/3.62 kg Painter Creek, Alaska 24 September 1985 Burton R. Leed
8 kg (16 lb) 5 lbs/2.26 kg Togiak, Alaska 10 September 1985 Robert L. Andreae
This is a good example of the results of a determined effort upon a previously vacant set of tippet classes—one angler, well prepared with certified scales, proper tippets, witnesses, camera, measuring tape and IGFA forms, in one week's fishing on one river, achieved almost a clean sweep. Now the job is to knock him off, in friendly fashion, of course.

GRAYLING: arctic (*Thymallus arcticus*) 5 lbs 15 oz/2.69 kg Katseyedie River, Northwest Territories 16 August 1967 Jeanne P. Branson
Line Class
1 kg (2 lb) 3 lbs 1 oz/1.38 kg Great Bear Lake, Northwest Territories 17 August 1983 Joseph B. Doggett
2 kg (4 lb) 4 lbs 10 oz/2.09 kg Great Bear Lake, Northwest Territories 9 August 1984 Carol P. Bull
4 kg (8 lb) 5 lbs 4 oz/2.38 kg Great Bear Lake, Northwest Territories 1 August 1986 Silvio Ronconi
6 kg (12 lb) 4 lbs 4 oz/1.92 kg Port Radium, Northwest Territories 21 August 1978 Raymond Goodrich
8 kg (16 lb) 3 lbs 5 oz/1.50 kg Casa-de-Paga River, Alaska 25 September 1985 M. Shane Kirkland
10 kg (20 lb) 3 lbs 7 oz/1.55 kg Casa-de-Paga River, Alaska 25 September 1985 Jack P. Kirkland
Fly Rod - Tippet Class
1 kg (2 lb) 3 lbs 8 oz/1.60 kg Great Slave Lake, Northwest Territories 6 September 1984 Don L. Guhlke
2 kg (4 lb) 3 lbs 8 oz/1.58 kg Great Bear Lake, Northwest Territories 18 August 1983 Joseph B. Doggett
4 kg (8 lb) 3 lbs 8 oz/1.58 kg Kasba Lake, Manitoba 10 August 1982 Ian P. MacDougall
6 kg (12 lb) 3 lbs 3 oz/1.46 kg Ugashik River, Alaska 9 July 1985 Jim Teeny

6 kg (12 lb) TIE 3 lbs 4 oz/1.48 kg Ugashik River, Alaska 30 July 1985 Danielle Smith
8 kg (16 lb) 2 lbs 12 oz/1.24 kg Stark River, Northwest Territories 13 July 1984 Bud F. Garland

MUSKELLUNGE: (*Esox masquinongy*) 69 lbs 15 oz/ 31.72 kg St. Lawrence River, New York 22 September 1957 Arthur Lawton
Line Class
1 kg (2 lb) 6 lbs 3 oz/2.80 kg Lake Kishkutena, Ontario 16 August 1986 Michael J. Baranowski
2 kg (4 lb) 35 lbs 8 oz/16.10 kg Leech Lake, Minnesota 24 May 1980 Bill Golembeck
4 kg (8 lb) 39 lbs 2 oz/17.74 kg Allegheny River, New York 19 November 1982 Gary Donahue
6 kg (12 lb) 50 lbs/22.67 kg Lake Nosbonsing, Ontario 21 September 1983 Terry L. Bachman
8 kg (16 lb) 45 lbs/20.42 kg 1,000 Island lake, Michigan 26 July 1980 Dr. William H. Pivar
10 kg (20 lb) 48 lbs 9 oz/22.02 kg Pewaukee Lake, Wisconsin 19 November 1977 Joe Ehrhardt
15 kg (30 lb) 56 lbs 7 oz/25.59 kg Manitou Lake, Ontario 30 August 1984 Gene Borucki
24 kg (50 lb) 55 lbs/24.94 kg Moon River, Ontario 11 October 1981 Gary Ishii
37 kg (80 lb) 35 lbs/15.87 kg Lake of the Woods, Ontario 2 November 1985 Richard Zebleckis
Fly Rod - Tippet Class
All fly rod classes are VACANT

MUSKELLUNGE: tiger (*E. masquinongy x Esox Lucius*) 51 lbs 3 oz/23.21 kg Lac Vieux-Desert, Wisconsin/ Michigan 16 July 1919 John A. Knobla
Line Class
1 kg (2 lb) VACANT
2 kg (4 lb) 18 lbs 8 oz/8.39 kg Stevenson Dam, Pennsylvania 5 July 1983 Samuel Brisini, Jr.
4 kg (8 lb) 30 lbs 8 oz/13.83 kg Round Lake, Wisconsin 12 May 1976 Leonard S. Grunow
6 kg (12 lb) 25 lbs 12 oz/11.67 kg Lac Vieux Desert, Wisconsin 2 October 1981 Dave Gallagher
8 kg (16 lb) 23 lbs 15 oz/10.85 kg Lake James, North Carolina 17 October 1983 John Ray Effler
10 kg (20 lb) 31 lbs 14 oz/14.45 kg St. Lawrence River, New York 1 October 1979 George C. Pifer
15 kg (30 lb) 31 lbs 8 oz/14.28 kg White Sand Lake, Wisconsin 25 August 1983 Matthew C. Belan
24 kg (50 lb) 28 lbs/12.70 kg Eagle Lake, Ontario 2 August 1982 Mark A. Wright
Fly Rod - Tippet Class
4 kg (8 lb) 17 lbs 4 oz/7.82 kg Freehold, New York 29 July 1983 Paul A. Schmookler
6 kg (12 lb) 30 lbs 6 oz/13.80 kg St. Lawrence River, Quebec 20 October 1985 Michel D. Croteau
All other fly rod classes are VACANT

PERCH: white (*Morone americana*) 4 lbs 12 oz/ 2.15 kg Messalonskee Lake, Maine 4 June 1949 Mrs. Earl Small
Line Class
1 kg (2 lb) 2 lbs 8 oz/1.13 kg West Kingston, Rhode Island 28 September 1982 Albert S. Ferris
2 kg (4 lb) 2 lbs 4 oz/1.02 kg Nantucket Island, Massachusetts 18 November 1985 William M. Pew
4 kg (8 lb) 2 lbs 8 oz/1.13 kg Coonamessett Pond, Massachusetts 29 June 1985 Chris Salpoglou

6 kg (12 lb) 2 lbs 6 oz/1.07 kg West Kingston, Rhode Island 25 September 1982 Frances E. Ferris
Fly Rod - Tippet Class
All fly rod classes are VACANT

PERCH: yellow (*Perca flavescens*) 4 lbs 3 oz/1.91 kg Bordentown, New Jersey May 1865 Dr. C.C. Abbot
Line Class
1 kg (2 lb) 2 lbs 9 oz/1.18 kg Yuba Reservoir, Utah 5 July 1984 Ray Johnson
2 kg (4 lb) 2 lbs 11 oz/1.23 kg Yuba Reservoir, Utah 4 July 1984 Ray Johnson
4 kg (8 lb) 2 lbs 5 oz/1.05 kg Yuba Reservoir, Utah 6 July 1984 Ray Johnson
6 kg (12 lb) 1 lb 15 oz/0.87 kg Barbers Pond, Rhode Island 26 September 1986 Holly Kristen Ferris
Fly Rod - Tippet Class
6 kg (12 lb) 1 lb 4 oz/0.56 kg Pakwash Lake, Ontario 16 October 1985 Lawrence E. Hudnall
All other fly rod classes are VACANT

PICKEREL: chain (*Esox niger*) 9 lbs 6 oz/4.25 kg Homerville, Georgia 17 February 1961 Baxley McCuaig, Jr.
Line Class
1 kg (2 lb) 5 lbs 2 oz/2.32 kg Newport News, Virginia 16 October 1983 Max Tongier, Jr.
2 kg (4 lb) 5 lbs 11 oz/2.57 kg Schoolhouse Pond, Rhode Island 11 August 1981 Albert S. Ferris
4 kg (8 lb) 6 lbs 11 oz/3.03 kg Richmond, Rhode Island 13 April 1985 David A. Greene
6 kg (12 lb) 6 lbs 14 oz/3.11 kg Lee Hall Reservoir, Virginia 3 January 1982 Max Tongier, Jr.
Fly Rod - Tippet Class
1 kg (2 lb) 3 lbs 5 oz/1.52 kg Newport News, Virginia 12 April 1984 Max Tongier, Jr.
2 kg (4 lb) 4 lbs 4 oz/1.92 kg Lovell's Pond, Massachusetts 24 October 1985 Jeffrey Joiner
4 kg (8 lb) 2 lbs 14 oz/1.30 kg Newport News, Virginia 12 April 1984 Max Tongier, Jr.
All other fly rod classes are VACANT

PIKE: northern (*Esox lucius*) 46 lbs 2 oz/20.92 kg Sacandaga Reservoir, New York 15 September 1940 Peter Dubuc
Line Class
1 kg (2 lb) 23 lbs 4 oz/10.54 kg Great Horden Lake, Kentucky 8 January 1984 John Pearn
2 kg (4 lb) 24 lbs 2 oz/10.96 kg Furusund, Sweden 25 May 1986 Yngre Pettersson
4 kg (8 lb) 35 lbs 8 oz/16.10 kg Lake Frigon, Quebec 26 June 1984 Thomas N. Quinzi
6 kg (12 lb) 34 lbs 6 oz/15.62 kg Angso, Sweden 2 May 1983 Magnus Herou
8 kg (16 lb) 27 lbs 8 oz/12.50 kg Moon Lake, Quebec 20 October 1986 Vince MacDonell
10 kg (20 lb) 29 lbs/13.15 kg Colin Lake, Alberta 20 September 1985 David H. Tenney
15 kg (30 lb) 31 lbs/14.06 kg Black Lake, Saskatchewan 9 June 1986 Alan L. Grove
24 kg (50 lb) 30 lbs/13.60 kg Trosa, Sweden 2 May 1986 Bill Tenney
As a highly desirable and world-ranging gamefish, the northern pike's records show a classic leveling-off of size as line weights increase. The all-tackle record seems suspect today, being not only fully 12 pounds greater than anything else listed but also close to 50 years old. Yet pike of that size and even slightly larger are caught every year now in northern Europe and occasionally in the British Isles; they simply are not listed with the IGFA, perhaps because of certification problems.
Fly Rod - Tippet Class
1 kg (2 lb) 24 lbs 3 oz/10.97 kg Brabant Is-

land, Northwest Territories 31 July 1985 John A. Propp
2 kg (4 lb) 22 lbs 8 oz/10.20 kg MacKenzie River, Northwest Territories 27 July 1983 John A. Propp
4 kg (8 lb) 21 lbs 8 oz/9.75 kg Great Slave Lake, Northwest Territories 13 August 1981 John A. Propp
6 kg (12 lb) 17 lbs 8 oz/7.95 kg Great Slave Lake, Northwest Territories 18 July 1983 Mickey Anderson
8 kg (16 lb) 22 lbs/9.97 kg MacKenzie River, Northwest Territories 5 August 1980 Charles A. Resen

SALMON: Atlantic (*Salmo salar*) 79 lbs 2 oz/35.89 kg Tana River, Norway 1928 Henrik Henriksen
Line Class
1 kg (2 lb) 4 lbs 11 oz/2.15 kg Ausable River, New York 20 September 1986 Edward T. Monsoor II
2 kg (4 lb) 16 lbs/7.25 kg Lac Tremblant, Quebec 19 May 1984 Pierre Lefebvre
4 kg (8 lb) 25 lbs 13 oz/11.73 kg River Morrum, Sweden 22 May 1983 Bjarke Schmidt
6 kg (12 lb) 33 lbs 15 oz/15.40 kg River Namsen, Norway 7 June 1984 Rolf Hagstrom
8 kg (16 lb) 38 lbs 9 oz/17.50 kg River Namsen, Norway 3 June 1981 Borge M. Jensen
10 kg (20 lb) 40 lbs 1 oz/18.20 kg River Namsen, Norway 2 July 1984 Inge M. Storm
15 kg (30 lb) 30 lbs 2 oz/13.67 kg River Gaula, Norway 15 July 1986 Hakan Brugard
24 kg (50 lb) 4 lbs 12 oz/2.15 kg George River, Quebec 20 August 1984 Jack Fallon
Why did Jack Fallon, a highly experienced and world-traveling fisherman, choose to set a "world record" with a fish not even 10 percent of the weight of his line class? Not much glory there, surely, yet only he knows for sure. The outfitter who guided him on the George may have insisted upon it, as a way of getting his operation listed with the IGFA. Atlantic salmon records in North America are necessarily slanted towards the fly rod category because salmon may legally be caught only on flies. In Europe, any tackle goes, hence the larger Scandinavian fish in the freshwater section, most of which were taken on prawns (large shrimp) lashed to bait hooks and cast with spinning tackle.
Fly Rod - Tippet Class
1 kg (2 lb) 22 lbs/9.97 kg Alta River, Norway 28 June 1983 Darryl G. Behrman
2 kg (4 lb) 29 lbs/17.46 kg Alta River, Norway 30 June 1983 Darryl G. Behrman
4 kg (8 lb) 31 lbs 8 oz/14.28 kg Alta River, Norway 25 June 1983 Darryl G. Behrman
6 kg (12 lb) 44 lbs 12 oz/20.29 kg Moisie River, Quebec 4 June 1980 Leopold Miousse
8 kg (16 lb) 47 lbs/21.31 kg Cascapedia River, Quebec 16 June 1982 Donal C. O'Brien, Jr.
Atlantic salmon have traditionally been an upper-class fish, especially in Europe, where the aristocrats fished for them with flies almost exclusively, and there is a strong tradition of salmon fishing that goes back more than a century. Today's modern records, which date from the inception of IGFA's data-keeping, don't take into account the dozens—perhaps hundreds—of well-documented European salmon of 60, 70 and even 90 pounds that were taken before the 1960s.

SALMON: king (*Oncorhynchus tshawytscha*) 97 lbs 4 oz/44.11 kg Kenai River, Alaska 17 May 1985 Les Anderson
Line Class
1 kg (2 lb) 34 lbs 10 oz/15.70 kg Chuitt River, Alaska 6 July 1984 Robert E. Hamilton
2 kg (4 lb) 39 lbs 12 oz/18.11 kg Kenai River,

Alaska 31 May 1984 Craig S. Archer
4 kg (8 lb) 62 lbs 4 oz/28.23 kg Kenai River, Alaska 31 July 1984 Donald R. Cloyd
6 kg (12 lb) 67 lbs 4 oz/30.50 kg Kenai River, Alaska 31 July 1986 Michael J. Fenton
8 kg (16 lb) 77 lbs 8 oz/35.15 kg Kenai River, Alaska 18 July 1985 Jerry Downey
10 kg (20 lb) 84 lbs 4 oz/38.21 kg Cook Inlet, Alaska 14 July 1984 Ray Holten
15 kg (30 lb) 97 lbs 4 oz/44.11 kg Kenai River, Alaska 17 May 1985 Les Anderson
24 kg (50 lb) 81 lbs 4 oz/36.85 kg Deep Creek, Alaska 15 July 1985 Dale C. Anderson
37 kg (80 lb) 65 lbs/29.48 kg Kenai River, Alaska 24 July 1986 Max Pruett, Jr.
60 kg (130 lb) 45 lbs/20.41 kg Kenai River, Alaska 26 June 1986 Kristian Iverson
Why does the Kenai River hold so many king (and other Pacific) salmon records? The main reason of course is that it is one of the world's prime king rivers. Another, equally important, however, is that part of the Kenai water is accessible by road from Anchorage—highly unusual, as most of Alaska is bush and so out of reach of those who cannot fly in—and so the fishing pressure is enormous. Many fish plus many fishermen equals records.
Fly Rod - Tippet Class
1 kg (2 lb) 22 lbs 4 oz/10.09 kg Little Manistee, Michigan 29 August 1983 Kenneth R. Darwin
2 kg (4 lb) 29 lbs/13.15 kg Karluk River, Alaska 11 July 1984 Rod Neubert, D.V.M.
4 kg (8 lb) 52 lbs 8 oz/23.81 kg Chetco River, Oregon 10 November 1982 Bob Byers
6 kg (12 lb) 44 lbs 6 oz/20.13 kg Chetco River, Oregon 4 November 1982 Patt Wardlaw
8 kg (16 lb) 54 lbs 8 oz/24.72 kg Chetco River, oregon 24 October 1981 Ed Given

SALMON: chum (*Oncorhynchus keta*) 32 lbs/14.51 kg Behm Canal, Alaska 7 June 1985 Fredrick E. Thynes
Line Class
1 kg (2 lb) 15 lbs 7 oz/7.00 kg Fish Creek, Alaska 1 August 1986 Jeff Trom
2 kg (4 lb) 17 lbs 5 oz/7.85 kg Fish Creek, Alaska 1 August 1986 Martin Vanderploeg
4 kg (8 lb) 15 lbs 6 oz/6.97 kg Fish Creek Alaska 1 August 1986 Jeff Trom
6 kg (12 lb) 18 lbs 8 oz/8.40 kg Kilchis River, Oregon 12 December 1984 Richard A. Weber
8 kg (16 lb) 22 lbs 2 oz/10.03 kg Hakai Pass, British Columbia 23 June 1985 Scott Bergey
10 kg (20 lb) 25 lbs 2 oz/11.40 kg Ketchikan, Alaska 1 July 1985 Tracy McLean
15 kg (30 lb) 17 lbs 5 oz/7.86 kg Kilchis River, Oregon 21 November 1985 Richard A. Weber
Fly Rod - Tippet Class
1 kg (2 lb) 13 lbs/5.89 kg Pah River, Alaska 18 August 1986 Lawrence E. Hudnall
2 kg (4 lb) 12 lbs 11 oz/5.75 kg Alagnak River, Alaska 17 July 1983 Gary Hibler
4 kg (8 lb) 23 lbs 4 oz/10.54 kg Dean River Channel, British Columbia 19 August 1983 Rod Neubert, D.V.M.
6 kg (12 lb) 23 lbs 14 oz/10.82 kg Stillaguamish River, Washington 7 December 1985 Michael F. Graham
8 kg (16 lb) 21 lbs 2 oz/9.60 kg Kilchis River, Oregon 18 November 1984 Jimbo Fowler

SALMON: silver (*Oncorhynchus kisutch*) 31 lbs/14.06 kg Cowichan Bay, BC 11 October 1947 Mrs. Lee Halberg
Line Class
1 kg (2 lb) 15 lbs 4 oz/6.91 kg Juneau, Alaska 16 August 1986 Harvey Minatoya, MD
2 kg (4 lb) 15 lbs 15 oz/7.24 kg Kenai River, Alaska 4 September 1985 Pat K. Johnson

4 kg (8 lb) 19 lbs 8 oz/8.84 kg Situk River, Alaska 20 September 1984 Melvin E. Snook
6 kg (12 lb) 21 lbs 8 oz/9.75 kg Prince William Sound, Alaska 18 August 1984 Robert Dolphin, DVM
8 kg (16 lb) 20 lbs 8 oz/9.29 kg Kenai River, Alaska 24 September 1984 Carloss R. Kirkman
10 kg (20 lb) 30 lbs 12 oz/13.94 kg Salmon River, New York 12 September 1985 Bub Cornish
15 kg (30 lb) 24 lbs 10 oz/11.16 kg Lake Ontario, New York 7 September 1984 Tom Cornell
24 kg (50 lb) 17 lbs 4 oz/7.82 kg Kenai River, Alaska 14 September 1984 Paul W. Pearson
Fly Rod - Tippet Class
1 kg (2 lb) 12 lbs/5.44 kg Karluk River, Alaska 10 September 1982 Ken Hower, Jr.
2 kg (4 lb) 15 lbs 8 oz/7.03 kg Karluk River, Alaska 9 October 1981 Rod Neubert, D.V.M.
4 kg (8 lb) 17 lbs 8 oz/7.93 kg Karluk Lake, Alaska 11 October 1981 Rod Neubert, D.V.M.
6 kg (12 lb) 19 lbs/8.61 kg Karluk Lake, Alaska 20 September 1983 Kevin Becker
8 kg (16 lb) 12 lbs 4 oz/5.55 kg Togiak, Alaska 9 September 1985 Robert L. Andreae

SALMON: pink (*Oncorhynchus gorbuscha*) 12 lbs 9 oz/5.69 kg Moose & Kenai Rivers, Alaska 17 August 1974 Steven Alan Lee
Line Class
1 kg (2 lb) 10 lbs 4 oz/4.64 kg Karluk River, Alaska 13 July 1984 Rod Neubert, DVM
2 kg (4 lb) 7 lbs 8 oz/3.42 kg Sandspit, British Columbia 30 August 1984 Gordon Prentice
4 kg (8 lb) 11 lbs 8 oz/5.21 kg Karluk River, Alaska 13 July 1984 Rod Neubert, DVM
6 kg (12 lb) 12 lbs 9 oz/5.69 kg Moose & Kenai rivers, Alaska 17 August 1974 Steven Alan Lee
8 kg (16 lb) 10 lbs 2 oz/4.60 kg Snohomish River, Washington 13 September 1985 F. John Erickson
10 kg (20 lb) 7 lbs 13 oz/3.56 kg Kenai River, Alaska 12 August 1984 Jeff Trom
15 kg (30 lb) 6 lbs 5 oz/2.86 kg Kenai River, Alaska 5 August 1984 Fred Pentt
Fly Rod - Tippet Class
1 kg (2 lb) 10 lbs/4.53 kg Karluk River, Alaska 13 July 1984 Rod Neubert, D.V.M.
2 kg (4 lb) 11 lbs 8 oz/5.21 kg Karluk River, Alaska 10 July 1984 Rod Neubert, D.V.M.
4 kg (8 lb) 3 lbs 14 oz/1.75 kg Kanektok River, Alaska 8 July 1982 Joe Ganim
6 kg (12 lb) 6 lbs 13 oz/3.11 kg Salmon Creek, Alaska 31 July 1985 Bob Garfield
8 kg (16 lb) 5 lbs 10 oz/2.57 kg Buskin River, Alaska 28 July 1986 Terry Stockman

SALMON: sockeye (*Oncorhynchus nerka*) 12 lbs 8 oz/5.66 kg Situk River, Alaska 23 June 1983 Mike Boswell
Line Class
1 kg (2 lb) 10 lbs/4.53 kg Russian River, Alaska 15 August 1985 Glenn Quick
2 kg (4 lb) 10 lbs 15 oz/4.96 kg Russian River, Alaska 14 August 1984 Martin Vanderploeg
4 kg (8 lb) 12 lbs/5.44 kg Kenai River, Alaska 23 July 1984 Richard G. Kincaid
6 kg (12 lb) 11 lbs 3 oz/5.07 kg Kenai River, Alaska 8 August 1982 Warren C. Hoflich
8 kg (16 lb) 12 lbs 8 oz/5.66 kg Situk River, Alaska 23 June 1983 Mike Boswell
10 kg (20 lb) 12 lbs 2 oz/5.50 kg Kenai River, Alaska 29 August 1986 Galen (Skip) Perry
15 kg (30 lb) 12 lbs/5.44 kg Kenai River, Alaska 7 August 1984 Galen M. Perry
Fly Rod - Tippet Class
1 kg (2 lb) 9 lbs 1 oz/4.11 kg Newhalen River,

Alaska 4 July 1985 Bruce Gernon
2 kg (4 lb) 10 lbs 15 oz/4.97 kg Kenai River, Alaska 30 August 1986 Roberta J. Knapp
4 kg (8 lb) 10 lbs 3 oz/4.62 kg Kanektok River, Alaska 6 July 1984 Jim Teeny
6 kg (12 lb) 10 lbs 7 oz/4.73 kg Brooks River, Alaska 22 August 1983 Jim Teeny
8 kg (16 lb) 10 lbs 3 oz/4.62 kg Kanektok River, Alaska 5 July 1986 Walker L. Hughes

SHAD: American (*Alosa sapidissima*) 1 lbs 4 oz/ 5.10 kg Connecticut River, Massachusetts 19 May 1986 Bob Thibodo
Line Class
1 kg (2 lb) 7 lbs 6 oz/3.34 kg Delaware River, Pennsylvania 10 May 1984 Ronald Yates
2 kg (4 lb) 8 lbs 14 oz/4.02 kg Delaware River, New Jersey 29 April 1984 André Moirano
4 kg (8 lb) 11 lbs 1 oz/5.01 kg Delaware River, New Jersey 5 May 1984 Charles J. Mower
6 kg (12 lb) 11 lbs 4 oz/5.10 kg Connecticut River, Massachusetts 19 May 1986 Bob Thibodo
Fly Rod - Tippet Class
1 kg (2 lb) 7 lbs 4 oz/3.28 kg Feather River, California 30 June 1983 Rod Neubert, D.V.M.
2 kg (4 lb) 5 lbs 9 oz/2.53 kg Delaware River, Pennsylvania 9 May 1986 Dave Wonderlich
4 kg (8 lb) 6 lbs 7 oz/2.92 kg Yuba River, California 30 May 1981 Eugene W. Schweitzer
6 kg (12 lb) 3 lbs 13 oz/1.72 kg Indianhead River, Massachusetts 20 May 1986 David Pickering
8 kg (16 lb) 5 lbs/2.26 kg Columbia River, Washington 14 June 1986 William J. Harris

SHEEFISH: (*Stenodus leucichthys*) 53 lbs/ 24.04 kg Pah River, Alaska 20 August 1986 Lawrence E. Hudnall
Line Class
1 kg (2 lb) 24 lbs/10.88 kg Pah River, Alaska 19 August 1986 Lawrence E. Hudnall
2 kg (4 lb) 38 lbs 2 oz/17.29 kg Kobuk River, Alaska 12 September 1982 Mark Feldman, M.D.
4 kg (8 lb) 39 lbs/17.69 kg Kobuk River, Alaska 20 August 1986 Daniel J. Hudnall
6 kg (12 lb) 33 lbs 9 oz/15.22 kg Kobuk River, Alaska 29 August 1981 John A. Berg
8 kg (16 lb) 34 lbs/15.42 kg Kobuk River, Alaska 21 August 1986 Lawrence E. Hudnall
10 kg (20 lb) 53 lbs/24.04 kg Pah River, Alaska 20 August 1986 Lawrence E. Hudnall
15 kg (30 lb) 25 lbs/11.33 kg Kobuk River, Alaska 6 June 1986 Michael M. Hamrick
24 kg (50 lb) 25 lbs/11.33 kg Kobuk River, Alaska 19 August 1986 Daniel J. Hudnall
Fly Rod - Tippet Class
1 kg (2 lb) 16 lbs 8 oz/7.48 kg Hoholitna River, Alaska 23 June 1982 Edward J. Cramer
2 kg (4 lb) 13 lbs/5.89 kg Hoholitna River, Alaska 23 June 1984 Elmer M. Rusten
4 kg (8 lb) 11 lbs/4.98 kg Kobuk River, Alaska 28 August 1981 George Gehrke
6 kg (12 lb) 18 lbs/8.16 kg Pah River, Alaska 19 August 1986 Lawrence E. Hudnall
8 kg (16 lb) 17 lbs 9 oz/7.96 kg Kobuk River, Alaska 28 August 1981 Jim Teeny

SUNFISH: green (*Lepomis cyanellus*) 2 lbs 2 oz/0.96 kg Stockton Lake, Missouri 18 June 1971 Paul M. Dilley
All classes are VACANT

SUNFISH: longear (*Lepomis megalotis*) 1 lb 12 oz/0.79 kg Elephant Butte Lake, New Mexico 9 May 1985 Patricia Stout

SUNFISH: pumpkinseed (*Lepomis gibbosus*) 1

lb 6 oz/0.63 kg Mexico, New York 27 April 1985 Heather Ann Finch

SUNFISH: redbreast (*Lepomis auritus*) 1 lb 12 oz/ 0.79 kg Suwannee River, Florida 29 May 1984 Alvin Buchanan
Line Class
1 kg (2 lb) 1 lb 1 oz/0.48 kg Suwanee River, Florida 29 June 1986 Winston Baker
2 kg (4 lb) 1 lb 4 oz/0.56 kg Suwanee River, Florida 4 November 1984 Winston Baker
4 kg (8 lb) 1 lb 12 oz/0.79 kg Suwanee River, Florida 29 May 1984 Alvin Buchanan
6 kg (12 lb) 1 lb 2 oz/0.51 kg Suwanee River, Florida 23 July 1986 Bernard L. Schultz
Fly Rod - Tippet Class
All fly rod classes are VACANT

SUNFISH: redear (*Lepomis microlophus*) 4 lbs 13 oz/ 2.20 kg Merritt's Mill Pond, Florida 13 March 1986 Joey M. Floyd
Line Class
1 kg (2 lb) 2 lbs 2 oz/0.97 kg Alamance Lake, North Carolina 23 September 1984 Roy E. Jones
2 kg (4 lb) 2 lbs 12 oz/1.26 kg Conyer's, Georgia 22 June 1979 Loy P. Croker
4 kg (8 lb) 4 lbs 10 oz/2.09 kg Merritt's Mill Pond, Florida 23 May 1985 C.L. Windham
6 kg (12 lb) 4 lbs 13 oz/2.20 kg Merritt's Mill Pond, Florida 13 March 1986 Joey M. Floyd
Fly Rod - Tippet Class
1 kg (2 lb) 1 lb 4 oz/0.58 kg Merritt's Mill Pond, Florida 30 September 1986 Jerry Hill
2 kg (4 lb) 1 lb 14 oz/0.85 kg St. Johns River, Florida 1 November 1982 Marie Gardner
All other fly rod classes are VACANT

TROUT: brook (*Salvelinus fontinalis*) 14 lbs 8 oz/6.57 kg Nipigon River, Ontario July 1916 Dr. W.J. Cook
Line Class
1 kg (2 lb) 7 lbs 8 oz/3.40 kg Misstassini River, Quebec 1 September 1982 Bill Atwood
2 kg (4 lb) 8 lbs 4 oz/3.74 kg Minipi River, Labrador 9 August 1986 Parrie F. Willette
4 kg (8 lb) 6 lbs 8 oz/2.94 kg Lake Michigan, Wisconsin 30 June 1986 William H. Vance
6 kg (12 lb) 6 lbs 4 oz/2.83 kg Lake Michigan, Wisconsin 26 June 1985 Sharon E. Keas
8 kg (16 lb) 5 lbs 14 oz/2.66 kg Bee Lake, Ontario 14 August 1983 Stanley Schroeder
10 kg (20 lb) 4 lbs 3 oz/1.92 kg Ashuanipi River, Labrador 3 July 1986 Raymond Carignan
Fly Rod - Tippet Class
1 kg (2 lb) 8 lbs 4 oz/3.74 kg Minonipi River, Labrador 8 July 1980 Harvey S. Smith
2 kg (4 lb) 9 lbs/4.08 kg Little Airy Lake, Labrador 18 July 1981 Harvey S. Smith
4 kg (8 lb) 10 lbs 7 oz/4.73 kg Broadback River, Quebec 5 September 1982 James F. McGarry
6 kg (12 lb) Broadback River, Quebec 2 September 1986 Peter M. Baskin
8 kg (16 lb) 6 lbs 8 oz/2.94 kg Minipi River, Labrador 20 August 1986 Harry Robertson III

TROUT: brown (*Salmo trutta*) 35 lbs 5 oz/16.30 kg Nahuel Huapi, Argentina 16 December 1952 Eugenio Cavaglia
Line Class
1 kg (2 lb) 14 lbs 6 oz/6.54 kg White River, Arkansas 1 February 1986 Anthony J. Salamon
2 kg (4 lb) 27 lbs 9 oz/12.50 kg White River, Arkansas 27 June 1981 Stanford D. Shanker
4 kg (8 lb) 33 lbs 8 oz/15.19 kg White River, Arkansas 19 March 1977 Leon L. Wagoner
6 kg (12 lb) 34 lbs 6 oz/15.59 kg Bar Lake,

Michigan 16 May 1984 Robert Henderson
8 kg (16 lb) 21 lbs 5 oz/9.68 kg Lake Michigan, Wisconsin 7 August 1982 Bert Coltman
10 kg (20 lb) 24 lbs 12 oz/11.22 kg Lake Michigan, Michigan 1 July 1984 Gayle Hoenke
15 kg (30 lb) 17 lbs 10 oz/8.00 kg Stockholm Stream, Sweden 3 November 1983 Magnus Herou
24 kg (50 lb) 14 lbs 4 oz/6.46 kg Lake Ontario, New York 29 April 1986 Paul Loquasto

Fly Rod - Tippet Class
1 kg (2 lb) 10 lbs 9 oz/4.80 kg Tongariro River, New Zealand 6 July 1986 Tuhi Y. Thompson
2 kg (4 lb) 11 lbs 9 oz/5.26 kg Tongariro River, New Zealand 23 May 1985 Louie Denolfo
4 kg (8 lb) 27 lbs 3 oz/12.33 kg Flaming Gorge Reservoir, Utah 13 April 1978 Joe Butler
6 kg (12 lb) 12 lbs/5.44 kg Lake Michigan, Wisconsin 24 November 1984 Allan L. Gens
8 kg (16 lb) 4 lbs 11 oz/2.12 kg Ryan Creek, Wisconsin 8 June 1986 Martin Frame

TROUT: cutthroat (Salmo clarki) 41 lbs/18.59 kg Pyramid Lake, Nevada December 1925 John Skimmerhorn

Line Class
1 kg (2 lb) 9 lbs 14 oz/4.50 kg Pyramid Lake, Nevada 21 July 1984 Ray Johnson
2 kg (4 lb) 10 lbs 14 oz/4.95 kg Pyramid Lake, Nevada 21 July 1984 Ray Johnson
4 kg (8 lb) 13 lbs 8 oz/6.12 kg Pyramid Lake, Nevada 2 February 1986 Jose Silva
6 kg (12 lb) 11 lbs 12 oz/5.32 kg Pyramid Lake, Nevada 8 November 1985 John A. Gorzelny
8 kg (16 lb) 11 lbs 12 oz/5.32 kg Pyramid Lake, Nevada 16 February 1986 Robert C. Brunner
10 kg (20 lb) 11 lbs 6 oz/5.16 kg Pyramid Lake, Nevada 30 July 1984 Ray Johnson

Fly Rod - Tippet Class
1 kg (2 lb) 2 lbs 13 oz/1.27 kg Clearwater lake, Montana 17 August 1981 Burton R. Leed
2 kg (4 lb) 4 lbs 7 oz/2.01 kg S. Platte River, Colorado 18 April 1986 John W. Lueckel
4 kg (8 lb) 14 lbs 1 oz/6.37 kg Pyramid Lake, Nevada 4 April 1982 Donald R. Williamson
All other fly rod classes are VACANT

TROUT: golden (Salmo aguabonita) 11 lbs/4.98 kg Cooks Lake, Wyoming 5 August 1948 Chas. S. Reed

Line Class
1 kg (2 lb) 2 lbs 2 oz/0.96 kg Bridger Wilderness, Wyoming 6 August 1985 Burton R. Leed
2 kg (4 lb) 1 lb 6 oz/0.62 kg Wind River Range, Wyoming 12 July 1986 Donald J. Dinkel
4 kg (8 lb) 2 lbs/0.92 kg Popo Agie Wilderness, Wyoming 11 July 1986 Dan Thurmond
6 kg (12 lb) 2 lbs 11 oz/1.21 kg Thumb Lake, Wyoming 12 July 1986 Thomas L. Pierce
A remarkable coincidence—three freshwater records set on the same species in the same state in a 24-hour period.

Fly Rod - Tippet Class
All fly rod classes are VACANT

TROUT: lake (Salvelinus namaycush) 65 lbs/29.48 kg Great Bear Lake, NWT 8 August 1970 Larry Daunis

Line Class
1 kg (2 lb) 28 lbs 5 oz/12.84 kg Flaming Gorge Reservoir, Utah 31 October 1984 Ray Johnson

2 kg (4 lb) 31 lbs 8 oz/14.28 kg Flaming Gorge Reservoir, Utah 5 November 1984 Ray Johnson
4 kg (8 lb) 38 lbs/17.23 kg Great Bear Lake, Northwest Territories 25 July 1984 Hugh S. Dougan
6 kg (12 lb) 50 lbs 8 oz/22.90 kg Great Bear Lake, Northwest Territories 22 August 1984 Marco J. Zonni
8 kg (16 lb) 53 lbs 4 oz/24.15 kg Great Bear Lake, Northwest Territories 16 July 1986 Richard J. Simourd
10 kg (20 lb) 63 lbs 9 oz/28.83 kg Great Bear Lake, Northwest Territories 31 July 1986 Mike Kroening
15 kg (30 lb) 60 lbs 12 oz/27.55 kg Great Bear Lake, Northwest Territories 26 August 1985 Barbara Goforth
24 kg (50 lb) 50 lbs/22.67 kg Jackson Lake, Wyoming 8 July 1983 Mrs. Doris Budge
37 kg (80 lb) 34 lbs 1 oz/15.45 kg Flaming Gorge Reservoir, Utah 17 November 1984 Ray Johnson
If ever there were a record that seems easy to knock off, consider the 80-lb freshwater class. An even moderately determined effort by an angler visiting Great Bear Lake would likely result in a new entry in the books. Keep it in mind, next time you're in the Territories.

Fly Rod - Tippet Class
1 kg (2 lb) 13 lbs 8 oz/6.12 kg Wellesley Lake, Yukon Territory 12 August 1986 T. Jack Beeler
2 kg (4 lb) 17 lbs 8 oz/7.93 kg Granby Dam, Colorado 18 September 1983 Larry D. Sneith
4 kg (8 lb) 20 lbs 10 oz/9.35 kg Granby Dam, Colorado 18 September 1983 Larry D. Sneith
6 kg (12 lb) 17 lbs 7 oz/7.90 kg Granby Dam, Colorado 18 September 1983 Ken Berkenhotter
8 kg (16 lb) 9 lbs/4.08 kg Selby River, Alaska 16 August 1986 Lawrence E.

TROUT: rainbow (Salmo gairdneri) 42 lbs 2 oz/19.10 kg Bell Island, Alaska 22 June 1970 David R. White

Line Class
1 kg (2 lb) 18 lbs 4 oz/8.27 kg Cowlitz River, Washington 4 July 1981 Larry Johnson
2 kg (4 lb) 23 lbs 12 oz/10.77 kg Bowmanville Creek, Ontario 28 April 1984 Brett Elliott
4 kg (8 lb) 26 lbs 9 oz/12.04 kg Lake Pend Oreille, Idaho 18 October 1982 Robert E. Pugh
6 kg (12 lb) 29 lbs 1 oz/13.18 kg Skeena River, British Columbia 12 November 1976 Day B. Karr
8 kg (16 lb) 30 lbs 9 oz/13.86 kg Lake Pend Oreille, Idaho 6 May 1980 Jack Wilkinson
10 kg (20 lb) 31 lbs 5 oz/14.20 kg Lake Pend Oreille, Idaho 19 November 1983 Gilbert Norlen
15 kg (30 lb) 30 lbs 5 oz/13.74 kg Thompson River, British Columbia 5 November 1984 Buzz Ramsey
24 kg (50 lb) 18 lbs 15 oz/8.58 kg Portage, Indiana 23 July 1986 Jack A. Davis

Fly Rod - Tippet Class
1 kg (2 lb) 16 lbs 8 oz/7.48 kg Salmon River, New York 22 February 1982 Francis J. Verdoliva, Jr.
2 kg (4 lb) 19 lbs 13 oz/9.00 kg Little Calumet River, Indiana 6 September 1982 Roger D. Enyeart
4 kg (8 lb) 24 lbs 8 oz/11.11 kg Sustut River, British Columbia 22 September 1982 Bruce Gernon
6 kg (12 lb) 22 lbs 8 oz/10.20 kg Rogue River, Michigan 1 April 1981 Glen D. Peoples

8 kg (16 lb) 28 lbs/12.70 kg Skeena River, British Columbia 20 October 1985 Chuck Stephens

WALLEYE: (Stizostedion vitreum vitreum) 25 lbs/ 11.34 kg Old Hickory Lake, Tennessee 1 April 1960 Mabry Harper

Line Class
1 kg (2 lb) 10 lbs 6 oz/4.70 kg Branched Oak Lake, Nebraska 18 April 1984 Thomas G. Bitting
2 kg (4 lb) 18 lbs 4 oz/8.27 kg Little Red River, Arkansas 14 March 1983 Mark S. Wallace
4 kg (8 lb) 19 lbs 5 oz/8.75 kg Greers Ferry Lake, Arkansas 2 March 1982 Erma W. Windorff
6 kg (12 lb) 22 lbs 11 oz/10.29 kg Greers Ferry Lake, Arkansas 14 March 1982 Al Nelson
8 kg (16 lb) 18 lbs 4 oz/8.27 kg Greers Ferry Lake, Arkansas 12 January 1982 Howard L. Brierly
10 kg (20 lb) 15 lbs 2 oz/6.86 kg Columbia River, Oregon 16 July 1984 Dan Nelson

Fly Rod - Tippet Class
1 kg (2 lb) 1 lb 14 oz/0.85 kg Strammond Lake, Quebec 10 June 1986 Dave Wonderlich
2 kg (4 lb) 5 lbs 12 oz/2.60 kg Mistassini, Quebec 19 June 1983 Bill Atwood
4 kg (8 lb) 8 lbs 10 oz/3.91 kg Humboldt River, Nevada 6 June 1984 Paul E. Bezayiff
6 kg (12 lb) 1 lb 5 oz/0.59 kg Strammond Lake, Quebec 10 June 1986 Thomas Heffernan
8 kg (16 lb) 5 lbs 2 oz/2.32 kg Lake Erie, Ohio 22 September 1985 Ben Doepel

THE INTERNATIONAL GAME FISH Association **saltwater** line class records actually comprise two categories— men's and women's records. We list here simply the larger fish of each of the two categories for each line class. The IGFA does not genderize its saltwater fly rod records.

ALBACORE: (*Thunnus alalunga*) 88 lbs 2 oz/40.00 kg Gran Canaria, Canary Islands 19 November 1977 Siegfried Dickemann
Line Class
1 kg (2 lb) VACANT
2 kg (4 lb) 40 lbs 2 oz/18.20 kg S.W.Cortez Bank, Mexico 24 November 1982 Capt. Jerry Wells, Sr.
4 kg (8 lb) 37 lbs 7 oz/17.00 kg Hout Bay, South Africa 18 April 1984 Nick De Kock
6 kg (12 lb) 68 lbs 12 oz/31.18 kg Port San Luis, California 7 November 1984 Kevin J. Crow
8 kg (16 lb) 71 lbs 12 oz/32.54 kg Catalina, California 14 November 1984 Roy R. Ludt
10 kg (20 lb) 76 lbs/34.47 kg San Pedro, California 14 November 1984 Michael E. Bradley
15 kg (30 lb) TIE 76 lbs 8 oz/34.70 kg Avalon Bank, California 11 November 1984 Ronald E. Howarth
15 kg (30 lb) TIE 76 lbs 8 oz/34.70 kg Newport Beach, California 11 November 1984 Charlie Ridgeway
24 kg (50 lb) 83 lbs 12 oz/38.00 kg Miyake Island, Japan 20 January 1986 Yuji Sato
37 kg (80 lb) 88 lbs 2 oz/40.00 kg Gran Canaria, Canary Islands 19 November 1977 Siegfried Dickemann
It seems the southern coast of California hosted an inshore run of unusually large albacore in November of 1984—six different world records (including one ladies' mark not recorded here) were set then, in less than a week.
Fly Rod - Tippet Class
6 kg (12 lb) 26 lbs 2 oz/11.85 kg San Diego, California 15 July 1972 Les Eichorn
8 kg (16 lb) 27 lbs 8 oz/12.47 kg San Diego, California 15 August 1970 Charles Davis
All other fly rod classes are VACANT

BARRACUDA: (*Sphyraena barracuda*) 83 lbs/ 37.64 kg Lagos, Nigeria 13 January 1952 K.J.W. Hackett
Line Class
1 kg (2 lb) 29 lbs 12 oz/13.49 kg Key West, Florida 10 January 1985 Jim Anson
2 kg (4 lb) 32 lbs 8 oz/14.74 kg Key West, Florida 8 May 1985 Bill Riesenfeld
4 kg (8 lb) 51 lbs/23.13 kg Key West, Florida 28 December 1979 John M. Ahearn
6 kg (12 lb) 68 lbs 14 oz/31.25 kg Cairns, Queensland, Australia 26 September 1982 Marianne Pearce
8 kg (16 lb) 69 lbs 10 oz/31.60 kg Coral Bay, W. Australia 4 September 1984 Katherine Webber
10 kg (20 lb) 70 lbs 8 oz/32.oo kg Innifail, Queensland, Australia 3 August 1979 Anne See Poy
15 kg (30 lb) 76 lbs/34.47 kg Seychelles Islands 14 October 1976 Amhand Moosa
24 kg (50 lb) 83 lbs/37.64 kg Lagos, Nigeria 13 January 1952 K.J.W. Hackett
37 kg (80 lb) 67 lbs/30.39 kg Islamorada, Florida 29 January 1949 Harold K. Goodstone
Fly Rod - Tippet Class
1 kg (2 lb) 19 lbs 12 oz/8.95 kg Key West, Florida 17 January 1985 Pete Peacock
2 kg (4 lb) 25 lbs/11.33 kg Key West, Florida

2 March 1985 Pat Ford
4 kg (8 lb) 31 lbs 12 oz/14.40 kg Key West, Florida 31 October 1979 Dallas Howard
6 kg (12 lb) 37 lbs 12 oz/17.12 kg Key West, Florida 19 December 1978 Joe Machiorlatti
8 kg (16 lb) 37 lbs 4 oz/16.89 kg Key West, Florida 16 December 1975 Roy Terrell

BASS: Striped (*Morone saxatilis*) 78 lbs 8 oz/ 35.60 kg Atlantic City, New Jersey 21 September 1982 Albert R. McReynolds
Line Class
1 kg (2 lb) 10 lbs 6 oz/4.70 kg Governor's Island, New York 20 November 1982 Stephen Sloan
2 kg (4 lb) 40 lbs 8 oz/18.37 kg Cape Cod Bay, Massachusetts 25 May 1985 Christopher Van Duzer
4 kg (8 lb) 56 lbs 14 oz/25.79 kg Gay Head, Massachusetts 15 October 1981 Richard C. Landon
6 kg (12 lb) 66 lbs 12 oz/30.27 kg Bradley Beach, New Jersey 1 November 1979 Steven R. Thomas
8 kg (16 lb) 69 lbs/31.29 kg Sandy Hook, New Jersey 18 November 1982 Thomas J. Russell
10 kg (20 lb) 78 lbs 8 oz/35.60 kg Atlantic City, New Jersey 21 September 1982 Albert R. McReynolds
15 kg (30 lb) 71 lbs/32.20 kg Norwalk, Connecticut 14 July 1980 John Baldino
24 kg (50 lb) 76 lbs/34.47 kg Montauk, New York 17 July 1981 Robert A. Rocchetta
37 kg (80 lb) 66 lbs 8 oz/30.16 kg Plum Island, New York 9 July 1982 Dennis R. Kelly
Fly Rod - Tippet Class
4 kg (8 lb) 42 lbs/19.05 kg Sacramento River, California 30 May 1986 Ronald S. Hayashi
6 kg (12 lb) 64 lbs 8 oz/29.25 kg Smith River, Oregon 28 July 1973 Beryl E. Bliss
8 kg (16 lb) 51 lbs 8 oz/23.36 kg Smith River, Oregon 18 May 1974 Gary L. Dyer
All other fly rod classes are VACANT

BLUEFISH: (*Pomatomus saltatrix*) 31 lbs 12 oz/ 14.40 kg Cape Hatteras, North Carolina 30 January 1972 James M. Hussey
Line Class
1 kg (2 lb) 14 lbs 8 oz/6.57 kg Chesapeake Bay, Maryland 25 May 1983 John C. Borotka
2 kg (4 lb) 18 lbs 4 oz/8.27 kg Norwalk, Connecticut 4 October 1985 William E. Miklovich
4 kg (8 lb) 21 lbs 1 oz/9.10 kg Montauk, New York 13 November 1977 Jeff Schneider
6 kg (12 lb) 24 lbs 3 oz/10.97 kg San Miguel, Azores 27 August 1953 M.A. da Silva Veloso
8 kg (16 lb) 21 lbs/9.52 kg Oregon Inlet, North Carolina 3 December 1984 Peggy B. McCaskill
10 kg (20 lb) 24 lbs 8 oz/11.11 kg Nags Head, North Carolina 12 November 1971 Mrs. Rita Mizelle
15 kg (30 lb) 26 lbs 8 oz/12.02 kg Buzzards Bay, Massachusetts 6 September 1984 Bill Lake
24 kg (50 lb) 31 lbs 12 oz/14.40 kg Hatteras, North Carolina 30 January 1972 James M. Hussey
Fly Rod - Tippet Class
1 kg (2 lb) 14 lbs 6 oz/6.52 kg Martha's Vineyard, Massachusetts 19 October 1984 Danwin M. Purdy
2 kg (4 lb) 14 lbs 9 oz/6.61 kg Martha's Vineyard, Massachusetts 19 October 1984 Danwin M. Purdy
4 kg (8 lb) 18 lbs 6 oz/8.35 kg Martha's Vineyard, Massachusetts 22 October 1984 Gregory J. Essayan
6 kg (12 lb) 19 lbs 4 oz/8.73 kg Virginia

Beach, Virginia 6 November 1980 Larry Greene
8 kg (16 lb) 19 lbs 8 oz/8.84 kg Nags Head, North Carolina 10 December 1984 Garry M. Oliver

BONEFISH: (*Albula vulpes*) 19 lbs/ 8.61 kg Zululand, South Africa 26 May 1962 Brian W. Batchelor
Line Class
1 kg (2 lb) 11lbs 12 oz/5.32 kg Islamorada, Florida 4 September 1985 Crawford W. Adams
2 kg (4 lb) 13 lbs 1 oz/5.92 kg Islamorada, Florida 14 December 1985 John (Doc) Savage
4 kg (8 lb) 13 lbs 15 oz/6.32 kg Islamorada, Florida 9 April 1978 Dick Moeller
6 kg (12 lb) 16 lbs/7.25 kg Bimini, Bahamas 25 February 1971 Jerry Lavenstein
8 kg (16 lb) 12 lbs 10 oz/5.72 kg Islamorada, Florida 6 October 1983 Roy Guilbault
10 kg (20 lb) 17 lbs/7.71 kg Mabibi, Zululand 24 May 1976 Peter F. Mason
15 kg (30 lb) 19 lbs/8.61 kg Zululand, South Africa 26 May 1962 Brian W. Batchelor
Fly Rod - Tippet Class
1 kg (2 lb) 11 lbs 12 oz/5.32 kg Andros Island, Bahamas 15 March 1983 Rod Neubert, D.V.M.
2 kg (4 lb) 15 lbs/6.80 kg Bimini, Bahamas 17 March 1983 James B. Orthwein
4 kg (8 lb) 13 lbs 4 oz/6.01 kg Islamorada, Florida 6 November 1973 Jim Lopez
6 kg (12 lb) 14 lbs 6 oz/6.52 kg Islamorada, Florida 22 September 1985 Vic Gaspeny
8 kg (16 lb) 13 lbs/5.89 kg Bimini, Bahamas 4 March 1986 James B. Orthwein

BONITO: Atlantic (*Sarda sarda*) 8 lbs 4 oz/ 8.30 kg Fayal Island, Azores 8 July 1953 D. Gama Higgs
Line Class
1 kg (2 lb) 7 lbs/3.17 kg Block Island, Rhode Island 8 September 1985 Capt. Greg Dubrule
2 kg (4 lb) 13 lbs 13 oz/6.26 kg Barnegat, New Jersey 14 November 1982 Ross J. Giarratana
4 kg (8 lb) 12 lbs 3 oz/5.55 kg Dakar, Senegal 7 March 1984 Dr. J.P. Terrisse
6 kg (12 lb) 13 lbs 8 oz/6.15 kg Madeira Islands, Portugal 6 June 1980 Kurt Muskat
8 kg (16 lb) 12 lbs 2 oz/5.50 kg Dakar, Senegal 7 March 1984 Dr. J.P. Terrisse
10 kg (20 lb) 16 lbs 12 oz/7.60 kg Gran Canaria, Canary Islands 6 December 1980 Rolf Fedderies
15 kg (30 lb) 16 lbs 12 oz/7.60 kg Madeira islands, Portugal 6 December 1982 Winfried Hobelmann
Fly Rod - Tippet Class
1 kg (2 lb) VACANT
2 kg (4 lb) 6 lbs 9 oz/2.99 kg Edgartown, Massachusetts 18 September 1982 Danwin M. Purdy
4 kg (8 lb) 7 lbs 3 oz/3.26 kg Martha's Vineyard, Massachusetts 19 September 1983 Kib Bramhall
6 kg (12 lb) 9 lbs 12 oz/4.42 kg Manasquan Ridge, New Jersey 28 September 1978 John A. Kaye
8 kg (16 lb) 13 lbs 6 oz/6.06 kg Key West, Florida 30 November 1975 Al Polofsky

BONITO: Pacific (*Sarda spp.*) 23 lbs 8 oz/ 10.65 kg Victoria, Mahe, Seychelles 19 February 19 Anne Cochain
Line Class
1 kg (2 lb) 8 lbs/3.62 kg San Martin Island, Mexico 28 November 1982 Capt. Jerry Wells, Sr.
2 kg (4 lb) 10 lbs 2 oz/4.59 kg Narooma, N.S.W., Australia 9 March 1984 Rick Tracey

4 kg (8 lb) 13 lbs 2 oz/5.95 kg La Jolla, California 23 July 1983 Thomas W. Edmunds
6 kg (12 lb) 16 lbs 8 oz/7.50 kg Sir Joseph Young Banks, N.S.W., Australia 24 April 1979 Mrs. Aileen Malone
8.kg (16 lb) 13 lbs 7 oz/6.09 kg Balboa, California 14 July 1983 Bill Seiler
10 kg (20 lb) 21 lbs 3 oz/10.07 kg Malibu, California 30 July 1978 Gino M. Picciolo
15 kg (30 lb) 20 lbs 11 oz/9.40 kg Montague island, N.S.W., Australia 1 April 1978 Bruce Conley
Fly Rod - Tippet Class
1 kg (2 lb) 2 lbs 7 oz/1.10 kg Santa Monica Bay, California 6 November 1983 Roy Lawson
6 kg (12 lb) 15 lbs 8 oz/7.03 kg Monterey Bay, California 15 September 1972 Bob Edgley
All other fly rod classes are VACANT

DOLPHIN: (*Coryphaena hippurus*) 87 lbs/39.46 kg Papagallo Gulf, Costa Rica 25 September 1976 Manuel Salazar
Line Class
1 kg (2 lb) 24 lbs/10.88 kg Pinas Bay, Panama 7 May 1984 Linda L. Miller
2 kg (4 lb) 38 lbs/17.23 kg Cozumel, Mexico 4 April 1982 Robert Smallwood
4 kg (8 lb) 58 lbs/26.30 kg Mona Passage, Puerto Rico 26 May 1984 Luis A. Battistini, Sr.
6 kg (12 lb) 77 lbs 2 oz/34.98 kg Islamorada, Florida 2 January 1982 Monte W. Green
8 kg (16 lb) 56 lbs 12 oz/25.74 kg Key West, Florida 5 June 1984 Rita L. Pierce
10 kg (20 lb) 83 lbs 6 oz/37.81 kg Mazatlan, Mexico 24 April 1972 Mrs. Eugene W. Wooten
15 kg (30 lb) 77 lbs/34.92 kg Fort Pierce, Florida 22 May 1982 Luke Cain, Jr.
24 kg (50 lb) 87 lbs/39.46 kg Papagallo Gulf, Costa Rica 25 September 1976 Manuel Salazar
37 kg (80 lb) 77 lbs/34.92 kg Nags Head, North Carolina 3 July 1973 Louis Van Miller
Fly Rod - Tippet Class
1 kg (2 lb) 4 lbs 12 oz/2.15 kg Key West, Florida 1 May 1986 Herbert G. Ratner, Jr.
2 kg (4 lb) 17 lbs 12 oz/8.05 kg Pinas Bay, Panama 3 April 1983 Jorg Marquard
4 kg (8 lb) 34 lbs/15.42 kg Pinas Bay, Panama 23 December 1980 Tred Barta
6 kg (12 lb) 58 lbs/26.30 kg Pinas Bay, Panama 6 December 1964 Stuart Apte
8 kg (16 lb) 45 lbs/20.41 kg Tongue of the Ocean, Bahamas 17 December 1971 Harold Siebens

DRUM: red (*Sciaenops ocellata*) 94 lbs 2 oz/42.69 kg Avon, North Carolina 7 November 1984 David G. Deuel
Line Class
1 kg (2 lb) 12 lbs 13 oz/5.81 kg New Smyrna Beach, Florida 31 August 1986 David M. Fairbanks
2 kg (4 lb) 22 lbs 13 oz/10.34 kg Empire, Louisiana 13 March 1982 Maumus F. Claverie
4 kg (8 lb) 48 lbs 8 oz/21.99 kg Hatteras Island, North Carolina 6 June 1983 Elvin L. Hooper
6 kg (12 lb) 69 lbs 3 oz/31.38 kg Gwynns Island, Virginia 10 July 1975 John O. Everett
8 kg (16 lb) 60 lbs 4 oz/27.32 kg Avon, North Carolina 5 November 1984 Joan Hinson
10 kg (20 lb) 72 lbs 7 oz/32.85 kg Hatteras Island, North Carolina 27 November 1973 Wayne Plageman
15 kg (30 lb) 90 lbs/40.82 kg Rodanthe, North Carolina 7 November 1973 Elvin Hooper

24 kg (50 lb) 94 lbs 2 oz/42.69 kg Avon, North Carolina 7 November 1984 David G. Dueul
37 kg (80 lb) VACANT (minimum weight 68 lbs/ 30.84 kg)
Fly Rod - Tippet Class
1 kg (2 lb) 4 lbs 11 oz/2.15 kg Flamingo, Florida 28 September 1985 Carlos Solis
2 kg (4 lb) 10 lbs 8 oz/4.76 kg Flamingo, FLorida 27 August 1983 Jack R. Zitt
4 kg (8 lb) 24 lbs 12 oz/11.22 kg Ocracoke, North Carolina 27 April 1986 Stuart C. Lee
6 kg (12 lb) 42 lbs 5 oz/19.19 kg Oregon Inlet, North Carolina 12 May 1981 Chico Fernandez
8 kg (16 lb) 33 lbs 8 oz/15.19 kg Ocracoke, North Carolina 25 April 1986 Stuart C. Lee

MARLIN: black (*Makaira indic*) 1,560 lbs/707.61 kg Cabo Blanco, Peru 4 August 1953 Alfred C. Glassell, Jr.
Line Class
1 kg (2 lb) 24 lbs 4 oz/11 kg Cape Bowl;ing Green, Townsville, Australia 22 September 1985 Anne Dalling
2 kg (4 lb) 72 lbs 12 oz/33.00 kg Cape Moretown, Queensland, Australia 16 January 1985 Jack Erskine
4 kg (8 lb) 244 lbs/110.67 kg Pinas Bay, Panama 26 January 1976 Edwin D. Kennedy
6 kg (12 lb) 737 lbs 7 oz/334.50 kg Cairns, Queensland, Australia 16 November 1981 Michael J. Levitt
8 kg (16 lb) 399 lbs/180.98 kg Pinas Bay, Panama 17 December 1983 Lawrence H. Furman
10 kg (20 lb) 1,048 lbs/476.73 kg Cairns, Queensland, Australia 7 October 1976 Peter W. Mahood
15 kg (30 lb) 1,077 lbs/489.50 kg Cairns, Queensland, Australia 28 November 1980 Bob Oliver
24 kg (50 lb) 1,122 lbs/509.84 kg Cairns, Queensland, Australia 31 October 1969 Edward Seay
37 kg (80 lb) 1,347 lbs/611.00 kg Lizard Island, Queensland, Australia 1 November 1979 Morton D. May
60 kg (130 lb) 1,560 lbs/707.61 kg Cabo Blanco, Peru 4 August 1953 Alfred C. Glassell, Jr.
Fly Rod - Tippet Class
1 kg (2 lb) VACANT
2 kg (4 lb) VACANT
4 kg (8 lb) 46 lbs 4 oz/20.97 kg Cairns, Queensland 14 September 1972 William W. Pate, Jr.
6 kg (12 lb) 49 lbs 9 oz/22.50 kg Dunk Island, Queensland 3 October 1984 Andrew A. MacGrath
8 kg (16 lb) 42 lbs 6 oz/19.22 kg Cairns, Queensland 8 September 1972 William W. Pate, Jr.

MARLIN: blue, Atlantic (*Makaira nigricans*) 1,282 lbs/ 581.51 kg St. Thomas, Virgin Islands 6 August 1977 Larry Martin
Line Class
1 kg (2 lb) VACANT
2 kg (4 lb) VACANT
4 kg (8 lb) 143 lbs/64.86 kg LaGuaira, Venezuela 26 October 1986 Jerry Dunaway
6 kg (12 lb) 448 lbs/203.21 kg St. Thomas, Virgin Islands 6 September 1971 Frank L. Miller
8 kg (16 lb) 240 lbs 4 oz/109.00 kg Dakar, Senegal 13 June 1983 Michael Calendini
10 kg (20 lb) 430 lbs/195.04 kg St. Thomas, Virgin Islands 31 August 1970 Charles R. Senf
15 kg (30 lb) 604 lbs/274.00 kg Rio de Janeiro, Brazil 8 January 1986 Claus Buck-

mann
24 kg (50 lb) 830 lbs/376.48 kg San Pedro, Dominican Republic 16 February 1980 Randall Lama
37 kg (80 lb) 1,128 lbs/511.65 kg Hatteras, North Carolina 5 June 1975 Larry Martin
60 kg (130 lb) 1,282 lbs/581.51 kg St. Thomas, Virgin Islands 6 August 1977 Larry Martin
Fly Rod - Tippet Class
8 kg (16 lb) 96 lbs/43.54 kg Havana, Cuba 21 August 1978 William W. Pate, Jr.
All other fly rod classes are VACANT

MARLIN: blue, Pacific (*Makaira nigricans*) 1,376 lbs/624.14 kg Kaaiwi Point, Kona, Hawaii 31 May 1982 Jay. Wm. deBeaubien
Line Class
1 kg (2 lb) VACANT
2 kg (4 lb) VACANT
4 kg (8 lb) VACANT
6 kg (12 lb) 396 lbs 11 oz/179.90 kg Punta Colorado, Baja, Mexico 6 June 1981 Bernard A. Guentner
8 kg (16 lb) 632 lbs 12 oz/287.01 kg Pinas Bay, Panama 8 May 1984 Linda L. Miller
10 kg (20 lb) 768 lbs 10 oz/348.67 kg Buena Vista, Mexico 22 November 1982 Eugene A. Nazarek
15 kg (30 lb) 626 lbs/283.95 kg Pinas Bay, Panama 22 December 1983 Rinaldo Wenk
24 kg (50 lb) 1,062 lbs 8 oz/481.94 kg Kona, Hawaii 8 August 1986 Gil Kraemer
37 kg (80 lb) 1,014 lbs/459.94 kg Manta, Ecuador 12 May 1985 Jorge F. Jurado
60 kg (130 lb) 1.376 lbs/624.14 kg Kona, Hawaii 31 May 1982 Jay Wm. de Beaubien
Fly Rod - Tippet Class
All fly rod classes are VACANT

MARLIN: striped (*Tetrapturus audax*) 494 lbs/224.10 kg Tutukaka, New Zealand 6 January 1986 Bill Boniface
Line Class
1 kg (2 lb) VACANT
2 kg (4 lb) 110 lbs/49.89 kg Cabo San Lucas, Mexico 20 January 1986 Steve Reschke
4 kg (8 lb) 205 lbs/92.98 kg Cabo San Lucas, Mexico 3 April 1972 W. Matt Parr
6 kg (12 lb) 271 lbs 2 oz/123.00 kg Poor Knights Island, New Zealand 26 April 1981 Barry Hill
8 kg (16 lb) 262 lbs 5 oz/119.00 kg Stephensons Island, New Zealand 25 April 1982 Robyn Hall
10 kg (20 lb) 340 lbs/154.22 kg Bay of Islands, New Zealand 21 January 1977 Robyn Hall
15 kg (30 lb) 363 lbs 12 oz/165.00 kg Middleground, New Zealand 21 May 1983 Mark Gitmans
24 kg (50 lb) 494 lbs/224.10 kg Tutukaka, New Zealand 16 January 1986 Bill Boniface
37 kg (80 lb) 455 lbs 4 oz/206.50 kg Mayor Island, New Zealand 8 March 1982 Bruce Jenkinson
60 kg (130 lb) 398 lbs/180.53 kg Mayor Island, New Zealand 30 December 1974 John K. Boyle
Fly Rod - Tippet Class
6 kg (12 lb) 148 lbs/67.13 kg Salinas, Ecuador May 1967 Lee Wulff
8 kg (16 lb) 146 lbs/66.22 kg Salinas, Ecuador 10 February 1970 William W. Pate, Jr.
All other fly rod classes are VACANT

MARLIN: white (*Tetrapturus albidus*) 81 lbs 14 oz/ 82.50 kg Vitoria, Brazil 8 December 1979 Evandro Luiz Coser
Line Class
1 kg (2 lb) 87 lbs/39.46 kg Nantucket, Mas-

sachusetts 23 August 1986 Ron Nation
2 kg (4 lb) 97 lbs 4 oz/44.11 kg Nantucket, Massachusetts 2 September 1986 Susan C. Goodwin
4 kg (8 lb) 81 lbs/36.74 kg Montauk, New York 19 July 1975 Stephen Sloan
6 kg (12 lb) 122 lbs/55.33 kg Bimini, Bahamas 30 March 1953 Dorothy A. Curtice
8 kg (16 lb) 114 lbs/51.71 kg Nantucket, Massachusetts 1 September 1986 Biddy Pauley
10 kg (20 lb) 170 lbs 10 oz/77.40 kg Guarapari, Brazil 2 December 1978 Raul S. Francisco
15 kg (30 lb) 181 lbs 14 oz/82.50 kg Vitoria, Brazil 8 December 1979 Evandro A. Coser
24 kg (50 lb) 174 lbs 3 oz/79.00 kg Vitoria, Brazil 1 November 1975 Otavio C. Reboucas
37 kg (80 lb) 151 lbs 10 oz/68.80 kg Rio de Janeiro, Brazil 24 November 1984 Mauricio S. Paixao
60 kg (130 lb) VACANT (minimum weight 120 lbs/54.43 kg)
Fly Rod - Tippet Class
1 kg (2 lb) VACANT
2 kg (4 lb) VACANT
4 kg (8 lb) 73 lbs/33.11 kg La Guaira, Venezuela 22 September 1984 Pat Ford
6 kg (12 lb) 68 lbs/30.84 kg Ft. Pierce, Florida 23 December 1972 Dave Chermanski
8 kg (16 lb) 80 lbs/36.28 kg La Guaira, Venezuela 17 September 1975 William W. Pate, Jr.

PERMIT: (*Trachinotus falcatus*) 51lbs 8 oz/23.35 kg Lake Worth, Florida 28 April 1978 William M. Kenney
Line Class
1 kg (2 lb) 23 lbs 10.43 kg Sunshine Key, Florida 10 May 1986 Sherril J. Ruilova
2 kg (4 lb) 31 lbs 8 oz/14.28 kg Key West, Florida 23 November 1985 Newbert Kenyon
4 kg (8 lb) TIE 38 lbs/17.23 kg Key West, Florida 19 March 1972 Stuart C. Apte
4 kg (8 lb) TIE 38 lbs/17.23 kg Bimini, Bahamas 29 April 1985 John L. Still
6 kg (12 lb) 50 lbs/22.67 kg Miami, Florida 27 March 1965 Robert F. Miller
8 kg (16 lb) 37 lbs/16.78 kg Key West, Florida 27 August 1983 Jim Thomas
10 kg (20 lb) 50 lbs 8 oz/22.90 kg Key West, Florida 15 March 1971 Marshall E. Earnest
15 kg (30 lb) 51 lbs 8 oz/23.35 kg Lake Worth, Florida 28 April 1978 William E. Kenney
24 kg (50 lb) 49 lbs 12 oz/22.56 kg Stuart, Florida 7 December 1976 Mark R. Arnold
Fly Rod - Tippet Class
1 kg (2 lb) 9 lbs/4.42 kg Sugarloaf Key, Florida 13 April 1986 Del Brown
2 kg (4 lb) 10 lbs 14 oz/4.93 kg Key West, Florida 19 March 1984 Del Brown
4 kg (8 lb) 41 lbs 8 oz/18.82 kg Key West, Florida 13 March 1986 Del Brown
6 kg (12 lb) 31 lbs 7 oz/14.25 kg Key West, Florida 2 May 1983 Pete Peacock
8 kg (16 lb) 36 lbs/16.32 kg Key West, Florida 3 April 1985 Kenneth Marlin

SAILFISH: Atlantic (*Istiophorus platypterus*) 128 lbs 1 oz/58.10 kg Luanda, Angola 27 March 1974 Harm Steyn
Line Class
1 kg (2 lb) 65 lbs/29.48 kg Quintana Roo, Mexico 15 April 1986 Jerry Dunaway
2 kg (4 lb) 70 lbs 10 oz/32.05 kg Dakar, Senegal 31 July 1986 Jean-Paul Richard
4 kg (8 lb) 97 lbs 7 oz/44.20 kg Dakar, Senegal 28 June 1984 Gary J. Sherman
6 kg (12 lb) 112 lbs/50.80 kg Cancun, Mexico 6 June 1979 Gloria J. Applegate
8 kg (16 lb) 105 lbs/47.62 kg Key Largo,

Florida 20 March 1986 James E. Frasier
10 kg (20 lb) 127 lbs 13 oz/58.00 kg Luanda, Angola 30 March 1975 Mario Da Silva
15 kg (30 lb) 116 lbs 5 oz/52.75 kg Luanda, Angola 22 March 1972 Jose E.G. Vaz
24 kg (50 lb) 128 lbs 1 oz/58.10 kg Luanda, Angola 27 March 1974 Harm Steyn
37 kg (80 lb) 106 lbs/48.08 kg Ft. Lauderdale, Florida 3 April 1982 Jason Haddick
Fly Rod - Tippet Class
1 kg (2 lb) VACANT
2 kg (4 lb) VACANT
4 kg (8 lb) 54 lbs 7 oz/24.70 kg Dakar, Senegal 17 September 1973 Dr. Pierre Affre
6 kg (12 lb) 64 lbs 11 oz/29.35 kg Dakar, Senegal 22 September 1984 Andrew A. MacGrath
8 kg (16 lb) 75 lbs/34.02 kg La Guaira, Venezuela 18 September 1975 William W. Pate, Jr.

SAILFISH: Pacific (*Istiophorus platypterus*) 221 lbs/100.24 kg Santa Cruz Island, Ecuador 12 February 1947 C.W. Stewart
Line Class
1 kg (2 lb) 102 lbs 4 oz/46.38 kg Pinas Bay, Panama 8 March 1985 Jean-Paul Richard
2 kg (4 lb) 113 lbs/51.25 kg Pinas Bay, Panama 12 December 1982 Lawrence H. Furman
2 kg (4 lb) TIE 113 lbs/51.25 kg Pinas Bay, Panama 19 February 1986 Jean-Paul Richard
4 kg (8 lb) 168 lbs/76.20 kg Salinas, Ecuador 7 September 1974 Santiago Maspons
6 kg (12 lb) 171 lbs 8 oz/77.79 kg Pinas Bay, Panama 9 January 1976 Felipe Estrada E.
6 kg (12 lb) TIE 171 lbs 8 oz/77.79 kg Exmouth, Australia 11 January 1983 Vic Rayner
8 kg (16 lb) 140 lbs/63.50 kg Salinas, Ecuador 30 January 1983 Santiago Maspons
10 kg (20 lb) 193 lbs/87.54 kg Acapulco, Mexico 8 January 1978 Anthony T. Russo
15 kg (30 lb) 198 lbs/89.81 kg La Paz, Baja, Bexico 23 August 1957 Charles Kelly
24 kg (50 lb) 192 lbs 7 oz/87.28 kg Acapulco, Mexico 4 October 1961 W.W. Rowland
37 kg (80 lb) 199 lbs/90.26 kg Pinas Bay, Panama 17 January 1968 Carolun B. Steiner
60 kg (130 lb) 221 lbs/100.24 kg Santa Cruz Island, Ecuador 12 February 1947 Carl W. Stewart
Fly Rod - Tippet Class
1 kg (2 lb) VACANT
2 kg (4 lb) VACANT
4 kg (8 lb) 66 lbs/29.93 kg Bahia Pez Vela, Costa Rica 9 July 1982 Bob Stearns
6 kg (12 lb) 136 lbs/61.68 kg Pinas Bay, Panama 25 June 1965 Stuart Apte
8 kg (16 lb) 117 lbs 8 oz/53.29 kg Bahia Pez Vela, Costa Rica 13 August 1979 Bob Stearns

SEATROUT: spotted (*Cynoscion nebulosus*) 16 lbs/7.25 kg Mason's Beach, Virginia 28 May 1977 William Katko
Line Class
1 kg (2 lb) 10lbs 1 oz/4.56 kg Daytona Beach, Florida 16 April 1983 David M. Fairbanks
2 kg (4 lb) 10 lbs 12 oz/4.87 kg Ponce de Leon Inlet, Florida 12 April 1983 Ben L. Britton
4 kg (6 lb) 14 lbs 6 oz/6.52 kg Texas City Flats, Texas 17 November 1984 Viola J. Hernandez
6 kg (12 lb) 14 lbs/6.35 kg Ponce de Leon Inlet, Florida 10 August 1972 Allen K. Gibbens
8 kg (16 lb) 12 lbs 9 oz/5.69 kg Spruce Creek, Florida 9 March 1986 Lonnie L. Nelson
10 kg (20 lb) 16 lbs/7.25 kg Mason's Beach, Virginia 28 May 1977 William G. Katko

15 kg (30 lb) 15 lbs 6 oz/6.97 kg Jensen Beach, FLorida 4 May 1969 Michael J. Foremny
Fly Rod - Tippet Class
1 kg (2 lb) 4 lbs 5 oz/1.95 kg Merritt Island, Florida 26 December 1983 Troy J. Perez
2 kg (4 lb) 7 lbs 4 oz/3.28 kg Merritt Island, Florida 8 December 1983 Troy J. Perez
4 kg (8 lb) 8 lbs 12 oz/3.96 kg Banana River, FLorida 5 December 1974 Dave Chermanski
6 kg (12 lb) 9 lbs/4.08 kg Jensen Beach, FLorida 2 January 1972 Elwood Colvin
8 kg (16 lb) 12 lbs 7 oz/5.65 kg Indian River, Florida 5 March 1984 Sidney A. Freifeld

SHARK: blue (*Prionace glauca*) 437 lbs/198.22 kg Catherine Bay, N.S.W., Australia 2 October 1976 Peter Hyde
Line Class
1 kg (2 lb) 119 lbs/53.97 kg Shinnecock, New York 1 July 1983 Stephen Sloan
2 kg (4 lb) 184 lbs/83.46 kg Montauk, New York 7 October 1984 Stephen Sloan
4 kg (8 lb) 254 lbs 10 oz/115.50 kg E. Port Hacking, Australia 20 November 1983 Denis Pearce
6 kg (12 lb) 312 lbs/141.52 kg Montauk, New York 28 October 1983 John S. Walton
8 kg (16 lb) 416 lbs 10 oz/189.00 kg Botany Bay, Australia 3 November 1985 Jayson Heyward
10 kg (20 lb) 368 lbs 2 oz/167.00 kg Swansea, N.S.W., Australia 3 November 1984 Narelle Wanless
15 kg (30 lb) 437 lbs/198.20 kg Catherine Bay, Australia 2 October 1976 Peter Hyde
24 kg (50 lb) 393 lbs/178.20 kg Montauk, New York 8 September 1979 Roy Carpenter
37 kg (80 lb) 410 lbs/185.97 kg Rockport, Massachusetts 17 August 1967 Martha C. Webster
60 kg (130 lb) 400 lbs/181.43 kg Le Morne, Mauritius 17 October 1976 Philip Fleming
Fly Rod - Tippet Class
1 kg (2 lb) VACANT
2 kg (4 lb) VACANT
4 kg (8 lb) 114 lbs 12 oz/52.05 kg Shinnecock, New York 28 June 1980 Stephen Sloan
6 kg (12 lb) 107 lbs/48.53 kg Barnegat, New Jersey 12 June 1981 John A. Kaye
8 kg (16 lb) 111 lbs 8 oz/50.57 kg Shinnecock, New York 23 June 1980 Stephen Sloan

SHARK: mako (*Isurus spp.*) ,080 lbs/ 489.88 kg Montauk, New York 26 August 1979 James L. Melanson
Line Class
1 kg (2 lb) 12 lbs 5 oz/5.60 kg Cape Naturaliste, Australia 28 March 1984 Adrian A. Pike
2 kg (4 lb) 83 lbs 8 oz/37.87 kg Shinnecock, New York 25 June 1984 Stephen Sloan
4 kg (8 lb) 342 lbs/155.23 kg Port Hacking, N.S.W., Australia 22 September 1974 Norman R. Smith
6 kg (12 lb) 414 lbs 7 oz/188.00 kg Port Hacking, N.S.W., Australia 21 September 1980 Paul Caughlan
8 kg (16 lb) 451 lbs 15 oz/205.00 kg Broken Bay, Australia 7 October 1984 Peter Green
10 kg (20 lb) 725 lbs 5 oz/329.00 kg Swansea, N.S.W., Australia 25 November 1979 Neil Williamson
15 kg (30 lb) 854 lbs/387.37 kg Port Stephens, N.S.W., Australia 9 May 1971 John H. Barclay
24 kg (50 lb) 1,080 lbs/489.88 kg Montauk, New York 26 August 1979 James L. Melanson
37 kg (80 lb) 953 lbs 7 oz/432.50 kg Poor

Knights island, New Zealand   22 November 1983   Clyve Lamplough
60 kg (130 lb)   1,061 lbs/481.26 kg   Mayor Island, New Zealand   17 February 1970 James B. Penwarden

Fly Rod - Tippet Class
1 kg (2 lb)   VACANT
2 kg (4 lb)   VACANT
4 kg (8 lb)   37 lbs 7 oz/17.00 kg   Mt. Maun Gahui, New Zealand   25 January 1984 William W. Pate, Jr.
6 kg (12 lb)   43 lbs/19.50 kg   Manasquan, New Jersey 7 July 1979   John A. Kaye
8 kg (16 lb)   65 lbs/29.50 kg   Whakatane, New Zealand   21 January 1984   William W. Pate, Jr.

SHARK: tiger (*Galeocerdo cuvieri*)   1,780 lbs/807.40 kg   Cherry Grove, South Carolina 14 June 1964   Walter Maxwell

Line Class
1 kg (2 lb)   VACANT
2 kg (4 lb)   VACANT
4 kg (8 lb)   VACANT
6 kg (12 lb)   362 lbs 8 oz/164.42 kg   Islamorada, FLorida   1 April 1983   Andrew A. MacGrath
8 kg (16 lb)   526 lbs 14 oz/239.00 kg   Kendrew Island, Dampier, Australia   4 August 1984 Terry Coote
10 kg (20 lb)   907 lbs 3 oz/411.50 kg   Swansea, N.S.W., Australia   22 November 1981   Gary Hoff
15 kg (30 lb)   1,170 lbs 10 oz/531.00 kg   Cape Hawke, N.S.W., Australia   17 May 1986 Mick Volkens
24 kg (50 lb)   1,115 lbs 8 oz/506.00 kg   Broken Bay, Australia   31 March 1985   Mark Stevenson
37 kg (80 lb)   1,305 lbs/591.94 kg   Sydney, Australia   17 May 1959   Samuel Jamieson
60 kg (130 lb)   1,780 lbs/807.40 kg   Cherry Grove, South Carolina   14 June 1964   Walter Maxwell

Fly Rod - Tippet Class
All fly rod classes are VACANT

SHARK: white (*Carcharodon carcharias*) 2,664 lbs/1,208.38 kg   Ceduna, Australia   21 April 1959   Alfred Dean

Line Class
1 kg (2 lb)   VACANT
2 kg (4 lb)   VACANT
4 kg (8 lb)   VACANT
6 kg (12 lb)   96 lbs 10 oz/43.82 kg   Mazatlan, Mexico   30 April 1964   Ray O. Acord
8 kg (16 lb)   210 lbs 8 oz/95.50 kg   Swansea, N.S.W., Australia   29 October 1983   Gary K. Hoff
10 kg (20 lb)   1,068 lbs/484.44 kg   Cape Moretown, Australia   18 June 1957   Robert Dyer
15 kg (30 lb)   1,053 lbs/477.63 kg   Cape Moretown, Australia   13 June 1957   Robert Dyer
24 kg (50 lb)   1,876 lbs/850.94 kg   Cape Moretown, Autralia   6 August 1955   Robert Dyer
37 kg (80 lb)   2,344 lbs/1,063.22 kg   Streaky Bay, Australia   6 November 1960   Alfred Dean
60 kg (130 lb)   2,664 lbs/1,208.38 kg   Ceduna, Australia   21 April 1959   Alfred Dean

Fly Rod - Tippet Class
All fly rod classes are VACANT

SNOOK: (*Centropomus undecimalis*) 53 lbs 10 oz/ 24.32 kg   Parismina Ranch, Costa Rica 18 October 1978   Gilbert Ponzi

Line Class
1 kg (2 lb)   13 lbs 15 oz/6.34 kg   N. Miami, Florida   24 September 1983   Dick Fleming
2 kg (4 lb)   26 lbs 7 oz/11.99 kg   Miami Beach, FLorida 2 August 1982   Robert Janzer
4 kg (8 lb)   35 lbs/15.87 kg   Miami, Florida 16 April 1977   Gerald Hernandez

---

4 kg (8 lb)   TIE   35 lbs/15.87 kg   Rio Tulin, Costa Rica   8 January 1983   Alexander Madrigal
6 kg (12 lb)   43 lbs 8 oz/19.73 kg   Parismina Ranch, Costa Rica   11 October 1976   James Snyder
8 kg (16 lb)   34 lbs 8 oz/15.64 kg   Lake Worth, Florida   15 November 1985   Leonard Bryant, Jr.
10 kg (20 lb)   53 lbs 10 oz/24.32 kg   Parismina Ranch, Costa Rica   18 October 1978 Gilbert Ponzi
15 kg (30 lb)   43 lbs/19.50 kg   Lake Worth, Florida   18 May 1952   Lee K. Spencer
24 kg (50 lb)   44 lbs 3 oz/20.04 kg   Ft. Myers Beach, FLorida   25 April 1984   Robert De Cosmo

Fly Rod - Tippet Class
1 kg (2 lb)   3 lbs 9 oz/1.61 kg   Ft. lauderdale, Florida   28 December 1982   Mark E. Krowka
2 kg (4 lb)   5 lbs 12 oz/2.60 kg   Everglades, Florida   13 April 1985   Del Brown
4 kg (8 lb)   22 lbs 3 oz/10.06 kg   Sebastian River, Florida   24 July 1971   Dave Chermanski
6 kg (12 lb)   28 lbs 8 oz/12.92 kg   Stuart, Florida   10 July 1972   Martin Gottschalk
8 kg (16 lb)   26 lbs/11.79 kg   Barra del Colorado, Costa Rica   19 October 1980   Bill Barnes

SWORDFISH: (*Xiphias gladius*)   1,182 lbs/536.15 kg   Iquique, Chile   7 May 1953   L. Marron

Line Class
1 kg (2 lb)   VACANT
2 kg (4 lb)   VACANT
4 kg (8 lb)   109 lbs/49.44 kg   Pinas Bay, Panama   24 February 1984   Jerry Dunaway
6 kg (12 lb)   166 lbs/75.29 kg   Pinas Bay, Panama   21 February 1986   Jerry Dunaway
8 kg (16 lb)   243 lbs 8 oz/110.45 kg   Ft. Lauderdale, Florida   7 June 1984   Robert R. Goldsby
10 kg (20 lb)   310 lbs/140.61 kg   Palmilla, Baja, Mexico   24 May 1979   David G. Nottage
15 kg (30 lb)   392 lbs/177.81 kg   Nantucket, Massachusetts   3 August 1976   John F. Willits
24 kg (50 lb)   492 lbs 4 oz/223.28 kg   Montauk, New York   4 July 1959   Dorothea L. Cassullo
37 kg (80 lb)   772 lbs/350.17 kg   Iquique, Chile   7 June 1954   Mrs. L. Marron
60 kg (130 lb)   1,182 lbs/536.15 kg   Iquique, Chile   7 May 1953   L. Marron

Fly Rod - Tippet Class
All fly rod classes are VACANT

TARPON: (*Megalops atlanticus*)   283 lbs/128.36 kg   Lake Maracaibo, Venezuela 19 March 1956   M. Salazar

Line Class
1 kg (2 lb)   42 lbs 8 oz/19.27 kg   Key West, Florida   2 August 1986   Herbert G. Ratner, Jr.
2 kg (4 lb)   72 lbs/32.65 kg   Marathon, Florida   22 August 1985   Donald O. Renton
4 kg (8 lb)   147 lbs 6 oz/66.84 kg   Key West, Florida   26 March 1982   Anton G. Zukas
6 kg (12 lb)   178 lbs/80.74 kg   Key West, Florida   12 April 1986   Dr. Jeffrey L. Breslaw
8 kg (16 lb)   190 lbs/86.18 kg   Key West, FLorida   14 March 1986   Howard Ross
10 kg (20 lb)   243 lbs/110.22 kg   Key West, FLorida   17 February 1975   Gus Bell
15 kg (30 lb)   283 lbs/128.36 kg   Lake Maracaibo, Venezuela   19 March 1956   M. Salazar
24 kg (50 lb)   242 lbs 4 oz/109.88 kg   Cienaga Ayapel, Colombia 7 January 1955 Alfonse Salazar
37 kg (80 lb)   247 lbs 12 oz/112.40 kg   Port

Michel, Gabon   10 December 1980   Thomas F. Gibson, Jr.
60 kg (130 lb)   224 lbs 13 oz/102.00 kg   Port Michel, Gabon   22 December 1985   Didier Courteau

Fly Rod - Tippet Class
1 kg (2 lb)   14 lbs 14 oz/6.76 kg   Ft. Lauderdale, Florida   12 April 1983   Mark E. Krowka
2 kg (4 lb)   42 lbs 8 oz/19.27 kg   Marathon, Florida   12 May 1985   Bill Levy
4 kg (8 lb)   127 lbs/57.60 kg   Marathon, Florida   15 April 1985   Del Brown
6 kg (12 lb)   167 lbs/75.75 kg   Pine Island, Florida   1 June 1986   Dan W. Malzone
8 kg (16 lb)   188 lbs/85.27 kg   Homosassa, Florida 13 May 1982   William W. Pate, Jr.

TUNA: blackfin (*Thunnus atlanticus*) 42 lbs/19.05 kg   Bermuda   2 June 1978   Alan J. Card

Line Class
1 kg (2 lb)   7 lbs 14 oz/3.57 kg   Cozumel, Mexico   8 May 1983   Stephen Sloan
2 kg (4 lb)   27 lbs/12.24 kg   Key West, Florida 2 May 1983   Joan M. Garisto
4 kg (8 lb)   29 lbs 8 oz/13.38 kg   Challenger Bank, Bermuda   12 July 1982   Stephen R. Hutchins
6 kg (12 lb)   37 lbs 4 oz/16.89 kg   Northwest Edge, Bermuda   27 November 1982   Kevin K.R. Winter
8 kg (16 lb)   33 lbs 14.96 kg   Key West, Florida 13 May 1984   Irv Roger
10 kg (20 lb)   37 lbs 2 oz/16.83 kg   Challenger Bank, Bermuda   25 July 1977   Richard Simons
15 kg (30 lb)   38 lbs/17.23 kg   Bermuda   26 June 1970   Archie L. Dickens
15 kg (30 lb)   TIE   38 lbs/17.23 kg   Islamorada, Florida   22 May 1973   Elizabeth J. Wade
24 kg (50 lb)   42 lbs/19.05 kg   Bermuda   2 June 1978   Alan J. Card

Fly Rod - Tippet Class
1 kg (2 lb)   VACANT
2 kg (4 lb)   VACANT
4 kg (8 lb)   23 lbs 4 oz/10.54 kg   Key West, Florida   3 April 1983   Andrew A. MacGrath
6 kg (12 lb)   28 lbs 12 oz/13.04 kg   Key West, Florida   18 May 1983   Luis de Hoyos
8 kg (16 lb)   34 lbs 3 oz/15.50 kg   Islamorada, Florida   17 December 1977   Rip Cunningham

TUNA: bluefin (*Thunnus thynnus*)   1,496 lbs/679 kg   Aulds Cove, N.S., Canada   26 October 1979   Ken Fraser

Line Class
1 kg (2 lb)   VACANT
2 kg (4 lb)   VACANT
4 kg (8 lb)   41 lbs 8 oz/18.82 kg   Virginia Beach, Virginia   3 July 1977   Mrs. Wm. B. Duval
6 kg (12 lb)   68 lbs/30.84 kg   Montauk, New York   13 September 1983   William T. Collins, Jr.
8 kg (16 lb)   188 lbs/85.27 kg   Montauk, New York   5 September 1982   Stephen Sloan
10 kg (20 lb)   119 lbs/53.97 kg   Montauk, New York   9 September 1984   Stephen Sloan
15 kg (30 lb)   216 lbs/97.97 kg   Ocean City, Maryland   6 August 1977   Byron Phillips
24 kg (50 lb)   897 lbs 4 oz/407.00 kg   Gran Canaria, Canary Islands   25 March 1977 Charles Chtivelman
37 kg (80 lb)   1,116 lbs/506.21 kg   North lake, P.E.I., Canada   26 September 1985   Dr. J.M. Steffey
60 kg (130 lb)   1,170 kg/530.71 kg   North Lake, P.E.I., Canada   2 October 1978   Colette Perras, MD

Fly Rod - Tippet Class
1 kg (2 lb)   VACANT

2 kg (4 lb)   VACANT
4 kg (8 lb)   14 lbs/6.35 kg   Montauk, New York   30 August 1981   Stephen Sloan
6 kg (12 lb)   16 lbs/7.25 kg   Montauk, New York   29 August 1981   Stephen Sloan
8 kg (16 lb)   9 lbs 8 oz/4.30 kg   Montauk, New York   16 August 1966   Stephen Sloan

TUNA: yellowfin (*Thunnus albacares*)   388 lbs 12 oz/   176.35 kg   San Benedicto Island, Mexico   1 April 1977   Curt Wiesenhutter
Line Class
1 kg (2 lb)   12 lbs 5 oz/5.60 kg   Malindi, Kenya   28 February 1983   Dieter Weber
2 kg (4 lb)   19 lbs 13 oz/9.00 kg   Exmouth, Australia   26 July 1982   Ian P. Cornelius
4 kg (8 lb)   63 lbs 12 oz/28.91 kg   Moriches, New York   26 August 1978   Tred Barta
6 kg (12 lb)   163 lbs 2 oz/74.00 kg   Montague Island, Australia   15 May 1983   Phillip Volkens
8 kg (16 lbs)   173 lbs/78.47 kg   Kona, Hawaii   5 August 1983   J.O. (Hans) Cik
10 kg (20 lb)   213 lbs 13 oz/97.00 kg   Bellambi, N.S.W., Ausatralia   7 December 1980   Gregory P. Clarke
15 kg (30 lb)   245 lbs/111.13 kg   Kona, Hawaii   28 July 1978   Ann Blumenfeld
24 kg (50 lb)   361 lbs 10 oz/164.03 kg   Socorro Island, Mexico   6 December 1981   Jim D. Nemlowill
37 kg (80 lb)   388 lbs 12 oz/176.35 kg   San Benedicto Island, Mexico   1 April 1977   Curt Weisenhutter
60 kg (130 lb)   333 lbs 8 oz/151.27 kg   Clarion Island, Mexico   18 March 1981   Ralph A. Mikkelsen
Fly Rod - Tippet Class
1 kg (2 lb)   VACANT
2 kg (4 lb)   VACANT
4 kg (8 lb)   25 lbs 12 oz/11.68 kg   Challenger Bank, Bermuda   23 May 1986   James A. Pearman
6 kg (12 lb)   67 lbs 8 oz/30.61 kg   Bermuda   7 July 1973   Jim Lopez
8 kg (16 lb)   81 lbs/36.74 kg   Bermuda   28 June 1973   Jim Lopez

TUNNY: little (*Euthynnus alletteratus*)   27 lbs/   12.24 kg   Key Largo, Florida   20 April 1976   William E. Allison
Line Class
1 kg (2 lb)   15 lbs 4 oz/6.91 kg   Key West, Florida   1 May 1984   Pete Peacock
2 kg (4 lb)   16 lbs 8 oz/7.48 kg   Cancun, Mexico   15 June 1983   Joseph A. Webster III
2 kg (4 lb)   TIE   16 lbs 8 oz/7.48 kg   Key West, Florida   15 May 1984   Eileen Peacock
4 kg (8 lb)   21 lbs/9.52 kg   Cancun, Mexico   20 May 1980   Gloria J. Applegate
6 kg (12 lb)   24 lbs 15 oz/11.31 kg   Sea Bright, New Jersey   2 October 1977   Mark A. Niemczyk
10 kg (20 lb)   21 lbs 12 oz/9.86 kg   Islamorada, Florida   5 June 1979   John L. Morris
15 kg (30 lb)   27 lbs/12.24 kg   Key Largo, Florida   20 April 1976   Willaim E. Allison
Fly Rod - Tippet Class
1 kg (2 lb)   2 lbs 10 oz/1.19 kg   Challenger Bank, Bermuda   28 June 1986   James A. Pearman
2 kg (4 lb)   13 lbs 8 oz/6.12 kg   Key West, Florida   23 July 1983   Robert S. Bass
4 kg (8 lb)   18 lbs 4 oz/8.27 kg   Cape Canaveral, Florida   24 July 1972   Dave Chermanski
6 kg (12 lb)   17 lbs 12 oz/8.05 kg   Key West, Florida   18 May 1983   Luis de Hoyos
8 kg (16 lb)   18 lbs 8 oz/8.39 kg   Key West, Florida   2 June 1985   Jim Donnellan

WAHOO: (*Acanthocybium solanderi*)   149 lbs/ 67.58 kg   Cat Cay, Bahamas   15 June 1962   John Pirovano
Line Class
1 kg (2 lb)   VACANT
2 kg (4 lb)   34 lbs 6 oz/15.59 kg   Boynton Inlet, Florida   19 June 1986   Robert J. Sorg
4 kg (8 lb)   51 lbs/23.13 kg   Mayaguez, Puerto Rico   4 March 1978   Leroy V. Battistini
6 kg (12 lb)   81 lbs 7 oz/36.93 kg   North Rock, Bermuda   22 December 1984   Michael E. Midgett
8 kg (16 lb)   85 lbs 12 oz/38.91 kg   Mayaguez, Puerto Rico   10 June 1984   Luis A. Battistini, Sr.
10 kg (20 lb)   115 lbs/52.16 kg   Bermuda   2 July 1961   Leo Barboza
15 kg (30 lb)   108 lbs 9 oz/49.24 kg   Cape May, New Jersey   17 July 1977   Charlene Mascuch
24 kg (50 lb)   124 lbs/56.24 kg   St. Thomas, Virgin Islands   29 March 1967   Joseph H.C. Wenk
37 kg (80 lb)   139 lbs/63.04   Marathon, Florida   18 May 1960   George Von Hoffmann
60 kg (130 lb)   149 lbs/67.58 kg   Cat Cay, Bahamas   15 June 1962   John Pirovano
Fly Rod - Tippet Class
1 kg (2 lb)   VACANT
2 kg (4 lb)   VACANT
4 kg (8 lb)   17 lbs 10 oz/7.99 kg   Isla Coiba, Panama   12 October 1975   Stuart Apte
6 kg (12 lb)   16 lbs 8 oz/7.48 kg   Isla Coiba, Panama   12 October 1975   Stuart Apte
8 kg (16 lb)   28 lbs 12 oz/13.04 kg   Key West, Florida   15 April 1982   Jim Anson

WEAKFISH: (*Cynoscion regalis*)   19 lbs 2 oz/ 8.67 kg   Jones Beach Inlet, New York   11 October 1984   Dennis R. Rooney
Line Class
1 kg (2 lb)   11 lbs 12 oz/5.32 kg   Chesapeake Bay, Virginia   16 May 1982   Ellyson S. Robinson III
2 kg (4 lb)   14 lbs 5 oz/6.49 kg   Cape May, New Jersey   25 May 1986   Matthew D. Welsh
4 kg (8 lb)   19 lbs 2 oz/8.67 kg   Jones Beach Inlet, New York   11 October 1984   Dennis R. Rooney
6 kg (12 lb)   17 lbs 14 oz/8.10 kg   Rye, New York   31 May 1980   William N. Herrold
8 kg (16 lb)   17 lbs 14 oz/8.10 kg   Bridgeport, Connecticut   13 September 1986   June Andrejko
10 kg (20 lb)   19 lbs/8.61 kg   Chesapeake Bay, Virginia   19 May 1983   Philip W. Halstead
15 kg (30 lb)   16 lbs 9 oz/7.51 kg   Fire Island, New York   4 October 1985   Al Lorenzetti
15 kg (30 lb)   TIE   16 lbs 9 oz/7.51 kg   Chesapeake Bay, Virginia   16 May 1986   James E. Lester, Jr.
Fly Rod - Tippet Class
1 kg (2 lb)   VACANT
2 kg (4 lb)   7 lbs 11 oz/3.48 kg   Fairfield, Connecticut   1 August 1984   A.J. Hand
4 kg (8 lb)   10 lbs 4 oz/4.64 kg   Cape May, New jersey   6 July 1980   Gary L. Rudy
6 kg (12 lb)   10 lbs 11 oz/4.84 kg   Chesapeake Bay, Virginia   28 May 1983   Lawrence E. Haack
8 kg (16 lb)   11 lbs 2 oz/5.06 kg   Loyd Point, New York   13 July 1985   Howard F. Guja